REDHANDED

REDHANDED

SURUTHI BALA AND HANNAH MAGUIRE

AN EXPLORATION OF CRIMINALS, CANNIBALS, CULTS, AND WHAT MAKES A KILLER TICK

RUNNING PRESS

PHILADELPHIA

Running Press
Hachette Book Group
1290 Avenue of the Americas, New York, NY 10104
www.runningpress.com
@Running_Press

Printed in the United States of America

First Edition: September 2021

Published by Running Press, an imprint of Perseus Books, LLC,
a subsidiary of Hachette Book Group, Inc. The Running Press name
and logo is a trademark of the Hachette Book Group.

Print book cover and interior design by Susan Van Horn.

Library of Congress Control Number: 2021932908

ISBNs: 978-0-7624-7379-3 (hardcover), 978-0-7624-7380-9 (ebook)

LSC-C

Printing 1, 2021

*For my family, who patiently
put up with me while I wrote.
And for all you Spooky Bitches who
made this book possible.*

—SURUTHI

*For my sister, Isabel, without whom I
would have run away to Nepal to live as a goat.
And for all the Spooky Bitches who have
changed my life forever.*

—HANNAH

Contents

REDHANDED

Introduction

HELLO, READER. WE'RE GOING TO GUESS THAT YOU'VE PICKED up this book either because you're a Spooky Bitch and avid listener of *RedHanded*, the podcast . . . or because you're just a bit morbidly curious.

Either way, clearly you have great taste.

And if we've read you right, you'll probably be very much on board with what's to come, since this book is a deep dive into the extremes of human behavior, as shown by everyone's favorite mass murderers, serial killers, and general bad-news Berthas.

Chapter by chapter, we're going to delve into some of the most brutal murders from across the world and ask the obvious question at the heart of them all: What makes a killer tick? But before we get to that, let's get better acquainted.

In 2017, two twentysomethings happened to meet at a party. Suruthi Bala had just gotten back to the UK after a year of traveling, during which time she had discovered the magic of true crime podcasts. These podcasts had accompanied her on all those 27-hour-long bus journeys across Asia and solo hikes around South America, and served as a welcome distraction from all the dodgy tummies, mosquito bites, and motorbike crashes. After this trip, Suruthi was set to return to the exciting world of corporate conference production, in all its high-stress, high–jet lag glory—but first, to get herself back into the swing of life at home, she was saying *yes* to anything and everything. It was one such *yes* that led her to a party in deepest East London that November night.

At this party was Hannah Maguire; she was whipping up a vegan Thanksgiving dream feast for her American housemate and his entire extended family (all of whom were crammed into her tiny flat for the holidays). Story-loving, supremely dyslexic Hannah had fallen in love with podcasts while living in Korea *(South, don't panic)* and avoiding the snotty children she was supposed to be teaching English. By the time of the fateful Veegs-giving, Hannah was back in London, living the dream working in commercial musical theater, washing other people's crusty mugs and frequently napping at the back of the dress circle. She made almost no money doing this, which is how Hannah ended up in a house share overrun with Americans on air beds.

Over aquafaba meringues, the two ladies struck up the usual polite chitchat one makes with a random they don't know at a party. But as they sipped their wine, they discovered a surprising shared obsession with the case of JonBenét Ramsey. As they drank more wine, they did the very drunk-ladies-in-the-bathroom thing of promising to become best friends and open up a dogs-only ice cream shop—*or* start a true crime podcast together.

Sadly, Cones and Bones never came to be, but Hannah and Suruthi did meet up again—this time at the Blind Beggar pub on Whitechapel Road, the infamous hangout of the notorious Kray twins. Hannah and Suruthi hit it off again, and, realizing that they were both desperate for a creative outlet, decided to start that true crime podcast. And with that, *RedHanded* was born.

At first it was just meant to be a bit of a hobby; neither woman had any experience whatsoever in the world of true crime, podcasting, broadcasting, sound editing, audio production, research, or script writing. But why let small details like that stop you when you can buy a mic for £10 and talk about murder in the cupboard under your stairs with a total stranger?

Fast-forward to today, and *RedHanded* is an internationally renowned, award-winning, hit podcast with thousands of self-proclaimed Spooky Bitches tuning in for their weekly dose of murder, wit, and WTFs. But despite how far it has come, *RedHanded* continues to transport listeners back to that first-ever party at which Suruthi and Hannah sat together engrossed, discussing a case that fascinated them.

Week in and week out, we at *RedHanded* explore a veritable smorgasbord of murder cases with the aim of dissecting not only the story, but also the social, cultural, political, and psychological aspects that feed into every crime. During our years of research and exploration into the world of violent offenders, we have seen it all, but we keep coming back to one question: What drives a killer to kill?

And while the nature versus nurture debate has started to feel a little outdated—because the answer is of course *both*—we're fascinated by the mind-bending interplay between genetics, environment, and experiences, and how they impact who we are.

So after getting a few hundred podcast episodes under our belt, we decided it was time to pull together everything we'd learned and write this book about what sets a killer apart from the rest of us.

The answer to this question is of course incredibly complex, and the path that leads someone to kill another human being is a complicated and twisty-turny one. If you listen to *RedHanded (once again, top marks)*, you'll know that no matter how bad some of these cases are, we never once refer to the killers as "monsters." To do so implies something otherworldly about them and conveniently removes such people from being our societal responsibility. It dehumanizes them. And that just doesn't make much sense to us, because what leads a person to deviance and depravity is usually something very human indeed.

So let's get started . . .

1

GENETICS

Bad Genes, Brunner's Boys, and Bundy's PCL-R

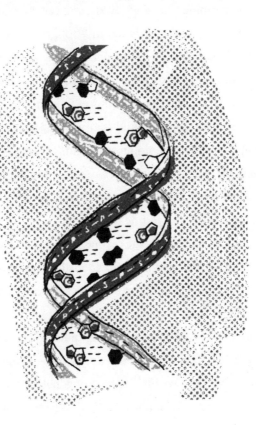

IN 2019, 26 MILLION PEOPLE TOOK AN AT-HOME DNA TEST. Compared to just four years earlier, that's a *1,633 percent* rise in people spitting in vials and swabbing their mouths to see if they can still eat bread or to find out just how Irish they are. We can't think of anything else that has grown in popularity that much recently. *(Except maybe true crime podcasts and craft avocado beer.)*

This astronomical rise in DNA testing shows us two things: our endless fascination with who we are *genetically,* and how the fields of genetics and molecular biology have evolved over recent decades. The first human genome, which was published in 2003, revealed some startling things—for a start, we have way fewer genes than anyone ever predicted! It also led to some amazing advances, like being able to screen for certain diseases, facilitating the discovery of incredible and novel therapeutics, making genome sequencing easy, and even making gene editing possible.

But what about the more complex elements of what makes us who we are, like personality and behavior? Can we simply take a look at someone's DNA sequence and predict that person's future, or are we just updating our tea leaves and tarot cards and calling it science?

These days it's hard to ignore the regular drumbeat of headline-making discoveries—claims that a gene has been identified for anything from procrastination to liberalism to adultery—and even for when a person will lose their virginity! *(We're not kidding.)*

So, what about a gene that predicts criminality? The notion that criminals are born rather than made is not a new one—since the 1930s, with the rise of new techniques within the field of genetics, the fervor to find a link between criminal behavior and genetics has been steadily ramping up. Why? Well, of course, if a genetic marker that predicted violence, depravity, and murder could be found, then perhaps interventions could be put in place; a person with that genetic vulnerability could be treated and maybe the future human cost of their offenses could be avoided. But we can't help but feel that there is also a flip side to this and the way it might offer some the chance to label killers "monsters."

If a clear genetic difference could be found between those who commit murder and the rest of us, wouldn't that be great? Wouldn't it mean then that they really are "other"? And wouldn't it be a huge relief, because then, we as a society could also stop worrying about taking any responsibility for the creation of these killers? After all, if these people are genetically predetermined to be murderers and criminals then we don't need to worry about inequality, poor housing, lack of access to healthcare, or substandard education systems—some people are just born bad.

We suspect that for some, such a simple premise would be ideal, but of course it's a lot more complicated than that, but stick with us; we're going to cram a lot of brain science down your throat in the next chapters as we explore the validity and the implications of the search for a "killer" gene . . .

Genes, Take the Wheel!

Let's start off by acknowledging that deciphering the interaction between genes and behavior is one of the most difficult tasks in biology. There is a lot of disagreement within academic circles over the science itself, and the topic of behavioral genetics, while fascinating, is often highly controversial. *(Like watching* Ancient Aliens *with supreme glee, while still knowing it's some racist bullshit.)* And it gets particularly dodgy when it comes to behavior (or even predisposition) linked to criminality.

There are many reasons for this societally, clinically, and legally, all of which we'll discuss in this chapter, but let's start with the legal side of things. Consider what it means to say that an individual is being driven to kill by their genes. It implies that the behavior isn't a choice and that it is out of their hands, and therefore the killer may not be responsible for their actions at all.

Bradley Waldroup: Born to Kill?

Let's explore this idea by heading to the mountains of rural Tennessee, where on October 16, 2006, Bradley Waldroup was sitting in his trailer home, waiting for his estranged wife, Penny, to arrive with their four kids who would be staying with him for the weekend.

The Waldroups recently had separated after several years of marriage, and Penny was obviously worried about what her husband was capable of. She had actually told her neighbor that if she wasn't back by seven thirty that night to call the police. And it appears that she didn't fancy dropping the kids off on her own, either, as she'd asked her friend Leslie Bradshaw to come along.

When Penny, Leslie, and the kids arrived at the trailer, Bradley met them holding a .22 rifle, and clearly he had been drinking. Penny hastily unloaded the kids' belongings. When the two women tried to get into their van to leave, Bradley said he wanted to talk. Penny desperately wanted to go; talking to her husband when he had been drinking was useless, so she said that she had to get to work but that they could talk when she returned to pick up the children.

But Bradley wasn't having any of it. He tore the keys to the van from Penny's hands and threw them into the woods, and then he began to scream at his wife. At this point, Leslie got out of the van and demanded that Bradley let them leave immediately and that he stop making a scene in front of the children.

8

Bradley was furious—as far as he was concerned, Leslie was the reason Penny had left him. Leslie was the one turning his wife against him. So, he picked up his rifle and opened fire on Leslie. Horrified, Penny got out of the van and ran, but suddenly she heard a crack of the gun and a bullet hit her in the back. Within seconds Bradley was on top of her; he had his pocket-knife out and he began stabbing Penny repeatedly. He then dragged her back toward the van, where he threw Penny down on the ground next to Leslie's body. Still seething with rage, Bradley proceeded to attack Leslie's body with a machete, slicing her head open. When Penny screamed at Bradley to stop, he slashed at his wife with the machete, chopping off her little finger.

He grabbed Penny by her hair and dragged her into the trailer. She was bleeding everywhere, so Bradley called for one of their daughters to bring her mother some water and towels for the blood. Bradley Waldroup then told all four of his children to come and say goodbye to their mother because it would be the last time they would see her.

Sobbing with fear and weak from blood loss, Penny kissed each of her children and told them that she loved them. Bradley Waldroup then told the bewildered kids to leave the room; he wanted to have sex with Penny. But he thought she was too messy and dirty *(you know, after he'd chased her, shot her, stabbed her, and cut her finger off with a machete)*, so he asked her to go and shower first. Penny refused; she wasn't going to make cleaning up after her own rape and murder easier for him. So, Bradley shrugged and forced Penny onto the bed and began to tear her clothes off.

Just then their daughter ran into the room saying that the police were outside. Penny, clad in just her underwear and bleeding from the gunshot and stab wounds covering her body, ran out of the trailer and jumped into the police car. She begged the officer to please go inside and save her children.

Thankfully, Penny Waldroup survived her harrowing ordeal, but her friend Leslie was already dead. Bradley Waldroup didn't put up any fight when the police approached him; he simply admitted to having attacked Penny and killed Leslie. In August 2008, prosecutors charged him with two counts of aggravated kidnapping, one count of first-degree murder, and one count of attempted first-degree murder. It seemed obvious to them that Waldroup's actions showed clear intent and premeditation. He had a gun and a machete to hand that day, and even if you disregard that, he told his children to say goodbye to their mother . . . he knew what he was going to do.

Remember: *Premeditation* doesn't mean you need to have sat down, worked out an intricate plan, and left the house with your murder go-bag and to-do list. It just means that during the commission of the offense, you had time to stop, think, and change your behavior. The very fact that Bradley Waldroup told Penny to take a shower so that he could rape her, to us at least, indicates that he was very much in control of what he was doing.

Prosecutors were certain that Waldroup would be found guilty on all counts and they wanted the death penalty. It was all absolutely horrific but seemed like a straightforward case. That is, until the case went to trial . . .

The Verdict

Following what had been a horrendously graphic four-day trial, the jury in the case of Bradley Waldroup deliberated for just 11 hours before reaching their decision. On March 21, 2009, audible gasps rolled around the courtroom as the verdict was announced: voluntary manslaughter. *Not* murder.

In an interview with NPR in 2010, prosecuting attorney Drew Robinson described how "flabbergasted" he was. It seemed unbelievable that a man who had shot a woman to death and then hacked up her body with a machete (and shot and brutalized his wife in front of their children) could have escaped a murder conviction. Especially in Polk County, Tennessee, which strikes us as a "tough-on-crime" kind of place.

So what had happened? Well, the answer lay in Bradley Waldroup's genes.

Waldroup's defense attorneys knew that they had to pull something out of the bag, so they went to forensic psychiatrist William Bernet of Vanderbilt University and asked him to give Waldroup a psychiatric evaluation. Bernet agreed, and he also took a blood sample to analyze Waldroup's DNA. As it turned out, Bradley Waldroup had just what the defense was looking for: he had the "warrior gene."

Monoamine Misadventures: The Warrior Gene

At the time of Bradley Waldroup's trial, the warrior gene was getting some serious media buzz and living its best headline-grabbing, spotlight-loving, *Dr. Phil*–special-appearing life. But to understand why people were absolutely losing their minds over this gene in the noughties, first we need to go back to 1978 and skip over to the Netherlands.

Because it was then and there that we'll find a Dutch woman who believed that there was something very wrong with five men in her family. A quick snapshot of what she was dealing with: one man was a serial arsonist, another had tried to run his boss over with his car, another had attempted to rape his own sister at knifepoint. Only one of the five had completed primary school and all of them had an IQ score lower than 85.

The Dutch woman sought out a clinical geneticist at the University Hospital in Nijmegen—Professor Han Brunner—and begged him to help her. She explained to Brunner that she felt the men in her family had some sort of hereditary issue that caused low intelligence and a propensity for extreme violence. And she hadn't been the first in her family to spot this pattern. Decades before, the woman's grand uncle had made a family tree and found even more men in the family that displayed these same traits, going as far back as the 1800s. This grand uncle was sure that there had to be some sort of genetic component that was causing his family's male violence problem; it couldn't be coincidence.

As it turned out, this woman and her grand uncle were right. In 1993 Han Brunner worked out what was going on: all of the violent men had a defunct variant of a gene called MAOA. It was an enormous discovery, as it was the first time that a specific gene had been linked to a human behavior like aggression.

So what was going on? Well, get ready, because we're about to take you on a magic school bus journey of science, junk science, and everything in between.

Genes are sections of DNA that provide instructions to make specific enzymes. MAOA is a gene that encodes the enzyme monoamine oxidase A. This enzyme breaks down the neurotransmitters (the brain's signaling molecules) serotonin, noradrenaline, and dopamine. If these neurotransmitters aren't degraded and removed when we're done with them, their buildup in the brain can lead to abnormal behavior and possibly aggression.

Naturally, the gene MAOA comes in several different forms, depending on the various levels of activity of the enzyme it regulates, monoamine oxidase A. Brunner's study found the males in that Dutch family had a variant of the MAOA gene that was completely inactive, so they had higher levels of noradrenaline, dopamine, and serotonin floating around their brains. Brunner theorized that the buildup of these molecules in the men's brains may have resulted "in over-excitation of the nerves in stressful situations," leading to their observably aggressive and hypersexual behavior. Brunner named this extremely rare condition Brunner's syndrome, and it's so rare, in fact, that this defunct, totally inactive variant of the MAOA gene has not been found outside of the men in that one Dutch family.

Another, and much more common, variant of the MAOA gene is MAOA-L (L for low activity), and this version leads to *less* monoamine oxidase A being produced. It's important to note that it's not a situation where none of the enzyme is being produced (like with Brunner's boys), just less than usual. And so those excess neurotransmitters like dopamine hang around in the brain for too long, but they *are* eventually removed, just at a slower rate.

And it is this variant—MAOA-L—that we are going to focus on now, because it is this version that went on to be dubbed the "warrior gene." (Why didn't the variant that the incredibly violent Dutch men had become known as the warrior gene, you ask? Well, again, because that variant so far has only been found in that one family. So to say it's rare would be a massive understatement.)

After Brunner's work suggested a link between the totally inactive MAOA gene and aggression, studies started rolling in on MAOA-L, and the hypothesis was that if a gene that produced *none* of this enzyme had been linked to such a strong tendency for aggression, then surely people with the less active variant must have at least a considerable propensity toward aggression.

No doubt some of these studies formed the basis of Bradley Waldroup's defense. It led to jurors convicting him of voluntary manslaughter rather than first-degree murder. When asked why they had voted the way they had, one juror told NPR, "A bad gene is a bad gene."

MAOA: No Way

So what does the science behind the controversial warrior gene actually look like? Well, a 2006 study—"Elevated Monoamine Oxidase A Levels in the Brain: An Explanation for the Monoamine Imbalance of Major Depression"—found that males with the MAOA-L variant had differences in their brain structure and function that could predispose them to aggression, specifically to *snap* while under pressure.

Research in this study focused on the brain structure in people with no history of criminality, violence, or childhood abuse. Brain scans revealed that those in the group with the MAOA-L variant were more likely to have smaller limbic systems than their non-MAOA-L study buddies. (The limbic system is a part of the brain that supports a variety of functions, including emotion, behavior, and long-term memory.) Researchers also found that there were some differences in brain activity; when the people with the MAOA-L variant were shown scary or threatening images, their amygdalas (the brain's emotional center that we'll meet in more detail later in this chapter) appeared to overreact. In particular, the males with the warrior gene were less able to inhibit their responses (i.e., they would physically respond).

OK, so this study was able to show brain differences in most people with the MAOA-L variant, but how do those differences actually manifest themselves? As super-hyper-aggression like the Brunner boys'? Well, not exactly.

For a start, roughly 40 percent of the general population has the MAOA-L variant! We think we can safely say that 40 percent of us aren't walking around bashing people's heads in, unable to control ourselves. *(Or shooting our wives and their friends . . .)*

In fact, in this study, it was found that 38 percent of the group had the warrior gene, yet none of those people had a history of criminality or violence. Remember, researchers specifically chose a group that was squeaky clean.

Now, it is worth mentioning that the scientists behind this study *did* state that the presence of the MAOA-L gene alone is not enough to predict violence, and that another trigger is needed. And of course, a typical trigger is having had an abusive childhood. So maybe one could argue that since the study had also chosen people who had no history of child abuse, that's why none of the subjects with the MAOA-L variant showed criminal tendencies or aggression.

Still with us? This brings us nicely to another study. A 2002 study looked at a sample of males who had all been maltreated as children to understand why some had gone on to develop antisocial behavior, while some hadn't. The researchers found that men with MAOA-L who had been maltreated were *more* likely to exhibit antisocial behavior than men with a similar background who had the normal MAOA gene. So the belief was that if a person has the MAOA-L variant *and* suffers an abusive childhood, they are at an increased risk of being aggressive and developing antisocial behavior.

Studies like this provided another string in the bow for Bradley Waldroup's defense. Waldroup had a very abusive childhood, and at his trial, his defense attorney certainly drew a connection for jurors between the abuse, Waldroup's warrior gene, and how Waldroup had exploded. In that 2010 NPR interview, one of the jurors summed up the defense's argument in one chilling statement: "Some people without this [the MAOA-L variant] would react totally different than he would. A diagnosis is a diagnosis."

Our jaws hit the floor when we read this. An abusive childhood in a killer's past is not something anomalous—as we'll see in our next chapter—and it rarely features as a significant mitigating factor at murder trials like this. Certainly not to the extent of reducing someone's conviction from first-degree murder to manslaughter. It's clear from the post-trial interviews that the "warrior gene plus abuse" argument was what had swayed these jurors. But as we'll see, the science is very much not there.

In 2014, along came the biggest-ever study of its kind—"MAOA Genotype, Childhood Maltreatment, and Their Interaction in the Etiology of Adult Antisocial Behaviors"—and it found that while childhood maltreatment was a significant risk factor for adult antisocial behavior, the MAOA-L variant had *no* effect!

Honestly, we could go on and on about this controversial gene and various studies, but our main point is just how *common* this variant is in the general population. We cannot stress this enough. And in fact, Professor Brunner himself pretty quickly distanced his work from suggestions that he had found a "gene for aggression."

At the Ciba Foundation Symposium conference in 1995, Brunner made it clear: "The notion of an aggression gene does not make sense, and it would be wrong to suggest that any one gene or collection of genes can account for something as complex as aggressive human behavior." He emphasized that his research has only demonstrated how a very specific genetic defect can result in a fairly specific behavioral abnormality in one particular family, not society at large.

And if you still have any lingering doubts, consider this: drugs that actually block monoamine oxidase A (the enzyme at the heart of this whole warrior gene business) have actually been used extensively to treat people with depression, and with no apparent increase in violent tendencies in those patients.

So is the warrior gene a likely predictor of violence? It doesn't appear so. At most, what some of these studies show is that people with the MAOA-L variant are more likely to be more reactive when threatened, but that's all. If nothing else, remember that a whopping 40 percent of people on average carry the variant, but only a *tiny fraction* of these carriers end up committing violent crimes. Most people with the warrior gene seem to make it through each day without totally fucking losing it and murdering another person. So to call these alleles "a gene for violence" is not just a massive exaggeration, it's just plain wrong. Genetics is a probabilistic science, and to say that one variant of a gene is responsible for the hugely complex human behavior of aggression and violence is a bit of a nonstarter.

The best we can say is that perhaps in some combination with other genetic and environmental factors, the warrior gene might impact one's ability to control any violent urges. But these factors most certainly do not predetermine a life of crime. And they absolutely do not remove criminal responsibility. The key takeaway is that no *singular* gene can determine criminality, violence, or murder-y desires. And as many scientists pointed out in the wake of Bradley Waldroup's trial, the notion that sentencing decisions should be made on the basis of such uncertainty is deeply, deeply troubling.

Waldroup, in our opinion, knew full well what he was doing. As we said, the MAOA-L variant is *at most* linked to increasing the likelihood of someone *snapping*, but Waldroup carried out a sustained attack that left one woman dead, one woman brutalized, and four children traumatized.

In 2010, a judge in Italy reduced the sentence of a man in jail for murder after it was found that he had the MAOA-L gene. Again, the scientific community was horrified, but if these sort of defense arguments continue to work, undoubtedly they will become increasingly common in our courtrooms—all the more reason to be careful before attributing complex behaviors to a single gene.

So now that we've shown you that the warrior gene doesn't really stand up to close scrutiny in terms of making a killer tick, let's go beyond aggression. Because to be honest, there are many other traits that make a "good" if not "better" killer: being unempathetic, manipulative, callous, charming, ruthless—sound familiar?

It's time to take a look at the personality disorder we all most readily associate with criminality and murder—*psychopathy*.

Maybe They're Born with It, Maybe It's Antisocial Personality Disorder

The whole contentious issue of the role genetics play in providing a predisposition for criminality takes a rather different turn when we consider psychopathy.

Over the last 20 years, in large part due to the work of Dr. Robert Hare, there has been a total shift in clinical circles from the idea that psychopaths are *created* by severe childhood trauma and abuse to the idea that psychopathy is mainly *genetic*. It is now generally agreed that psychopathy is a congenital state (i.e., you're born with it).

We know this because children start to show the signs of psychopathy from a very young age, and the traits tend to stay pretty stable throughout their lives. We'll go on to discuss the psychopathic child in more detail in chapter 2, but what is clear from Dr. Hare's research (like his 1993 study, "Psychopathy, Mental Disorder, and Crime") is that children with psychopathic traits are "inexplicably different" from other children—displaying aggression, manipulation, and deceitfulness from the very start.

Dr. Hare also states in his book *Without Conscience: The Disturbing World of the Psychopaths Among Us* that most of the psychopathic people he has worked with over the years did not report coming from abusive homes; in fact, the majority had grown up in relatively "normal" households with caring and supportive parents.

And so, given these findings, researchers went in search of *genetic* reasons to explain psychopathy. Although it is still not exactly clear *how* it is passed on, psychopathy is actually now considered to be the personality disorder with the highest genetic component. Studies like the 2014 paper "The Heritability of Psychopathic Personality in 14- to 15-Year-Old Twins" suggest that psychopathy is around 50 percent heritable, while the "Minnesota Twin Study" has shown that psychopathy is 60 percent heritable. There isn't an exact agreed upon figure, as you can see, but the general consensus is that psychopathic traits have a stronger relationship to one's DNA than to one's upbringing.

The key difference here is that no one is claiming—like with the warrior gene—that there is one singular gene for psychopathy. This would be massively wrong. There are likely a variety of genes, working in combination with differing brain structures, that correlate with psychopathic tendencies or behaviors.

We'll come back to what the brain structure of a psychopath looks like later in this chapter, but for now, let's talk about what exactly psychopathy is and how it's diagnosed.

Psychopaths and Where to Find Them

The word *psychopath* gets bandied about a lot these days, especially by the unqualified *(said the true crime podcasters)*. But are we using the term correctly? It has become so much a part of our lingua franca that a roommate leaving their dirty dishes in the sink overnight could earn themselves the title far too easily. Or, how many times have you dissected the behavior of your friend's "psycho" ex? We're all guilty of it, but as usual, most of us don't know what the hell we're talking about.

Psychopathy is possibly the most well-known but least understood personality disorder out there, so let's get into it . . .

We tend to use *psychopathy* and *antisocial personality disorder* (ASPD) interchangeably, but the best way to think about it is as psychopathy being a subset of ASPD. So what is antisocial personality disorder? ASPD is a Cluster B personality disorder, which means that it belongs to the *erratic* personality disorder family. Cluster B is also home to borderline personality disorder, histrionic personality disorder, and narcissistic personality disorder (more on these in chapters 5 and 6).

ASPD is a diagnosable condition, as it is listed in the American Psychiatric Association's *Diagnostic and Statistical Manual of Mental Disorders, Fifth Edition (DSM-5),* and it is thought to affect about 3 percent of the general population and around 80 percent of incarcerated populations. There are seven criteria, three of which must be met for a diagnosis: violating social norms; deceitfulness; impulsivity; irritability; irresponsibility; manipulative; and lack of remorse.

Psychopathy, on the other hand, is *not* a mental disorder, and as such it can't really be diagnosed. Psychopathy can be thought of as a construct, typified by a lack of empathy and callous behavior. And while ASPD is categorical (i.e., you have it or you don't), psychopathy is generally considered to be on a spectrum.

And what about sociopathy? Another term we tend to mix into this confusing soup of disorders. Well, sociopaths are generally considered to be created through abuse and trauma, unlike the genetic psychopath, and while many of us confuse the two terms given some similar behaviors—such as a lack of empathy, dishonesty, and shallow emotions—they are two very different constructs. Not just in terms of how they are formed in a person, but also because the sociopath, unlike the psychopath, is actually highly emotional (when it comes to negative emotions like rage) and likely to be very reckless. The best way to differentiate the two is to think of a cold, calculated, in control psychopath versus a hot-headed, volatile, impulsive sociopath.

Now that we've cleared that up, let's get back to psychopathy, and the specific traits that psychopaths display. Psychopaths are considered the most extreme citizens of the Antisocial Personality kingdom. They are usually charming, narcissistic, superficial, impulsive, callous, unemotional, and—like mean girls in high schools the world over—they have no problem throwing others under the bus to get what they want. Their only goal is the pursuit of pleasure, which, according to Lucy Foulkes in her study "Inverted Social Reward: Associations between Psychopathic Traits and Self Report and Experimental Measures of Social Reward," can be gained by hurting others, engaging in antisocial behavior, and being coercive and nasty.

That being said, despite what the Bateses and Batemans of Hollywood want you to believe, psychopaths *do* have feelings. They can feel excited or even happy, although the stakes have to be much higher than they would for a "normal" person. Crucially, guilt, anxiety, empathy, and remorse do

21

not make an appearance. According to Dr. Hare, a forerunner of the psychopathic research space, these "intraspecies predators" are not much fun to be around. Although they may understand the emotions of others, psychopaths don't tend to feel bad about any harm they cause. A guilt-free life may sound great, especially to the fallen Catholics among us, but having a psychopathic brain is by no means a one-way ticket to easy street.

Spot the Neurological Difference

One of the major differences between a psychopathic brain and a "normal"-looking one is in the function of the prefrontal cortex; there are also differences in brain structure. Researchers led by Dr. Michael Koenigs at the University of Wisconsin discovered, while examining the brains of male prisoners, that psychopaths have reduced connectivity between their prefrontal cortex and their amygdala.

This study, "Reduced Prefrontal Connectivity in Psychopathy"—which came out in 2011—was the first time "structural and functional differences in people diagnosed with psychopathy" were identified. Since you're reading this book, it's pretty plausible that you may have heard the terms *prefrontal cortex* and *amygdala* before. It's also highly likely that you heard those terms fall from the lips of Dr. Derek Shepherd on *Grey's Anatomy*, got distracted by his flowing locks, and aren't totally certain what they actually mean, but don't worry, we've got you.

The prefrontal cortex is the brain's control center and it's located right at the very front, just behind our eyes. It's responsible for executive functions like personality expression, decision-making, and moderating social behavior, but its main job is to control our emotional responses to stress. It functions kind of like an emergency brake or, according to neurocriminologist Dr. Adrian Raine, a guardian angel that stops us from making decisions we might regret.

The amygdala, often referred to as the brain's emotional center, is probably best known for its starring role in driving the fight-or-flight response, and as such it is associated with our responses to fear, stress, and anxiety. So, when you're filled with increasing existential dread when facing a looming deadline, a social engagement you don't want to be at, or another fuckboy appointment, that's your amygdala working its magic. *(So is the sweat imprint of your bum that you leave on the chair after a job interview. Thanks, amygdala.)*

The relationship between your amygdala and your prefrontal cortex is absolutely vital because it is believed to play a critical role in the regulation of emotion. How does it work? Well, the amygdala is there to detect threats in the environment, and when it spots one it sounds the alarm. The prefrontal cortex assesses the threat and then "tells" the amygdala whether the panicky alarm is proportionate. Essentially the amygdala is there to pick up on any biological or emotional stressors that may be dangerous (which is of course absolutely crucial to our survival), but the prefrontal cortex is there to course correct and calm the amygdala down so that we aren't all freaking out from stress and having meltdowns at the slightest threat.

When the connection between these two regions is weakened, it results in an individual's inability to regulate emotion and social behavior in a typical way. This can lead to the callous, unemotional, and unempathetic behavior we would expect from a psychopath.

What's also interesting is that while this brain structure seems to be congenital in a psychopath, this lack of communication between the prefrontal cortex and the amygdala can also be induced by a significant brain injury. See our sidebar on head injuries to learn more.

GAME-CHANGING
HEAD INJURIES

We've all heard stories about people having massive accidents and becoming total nightmares to be around—history's most famous being Phineas P. Gage, who you can read about in consultant neuropsychiatrist Kieran O'Driscoll's paper "No Longer Gage: An Iron Bar through the Head." The title of the paper gives the game away—Gage had a 1.1-meter-long tamping iron wedged in his skull in an 1848 accident and he miraculously survived, but his personality didn't. Before he took an iron bar to the prefrontal cortex, he had been a perfectly nice person. After the accident he was belligerent, irreverent, profane, and didn't care about anyone but himself.

As we will see in chapter 2, a *lot* of prolific serial killers sustained serious head traumas as children. If you have even a cursory interest in the National Football League and the sport that we like to call "American hand-egg" (known to many of you as American football), you may be aware of the devastating effects of the degenerative brain disease chronic traumatic encephalopathy (CTE).

Only diagnosable after death, CTE is understood to be a result of repeated blows to the head and repeated concussions, such as those sustained in contact sports. In possibly one of the most harrowing cases of this condition, Aaron Hernandez, a former New England Patriots football player, murdered Odin Lloyd in 2013 before hanging himself in prison at the age of 27. When his brain was examined, according to the *Washington Post,* he was found to have "suffered from the most severe CTE ever found in a person his age." And while one can't say definitively that CTE caused him to kill, it certainly would have influenced Hernandez's ability to manage his impulse control, decision-making, aggression, and rage.

Testing Psychopaths

Criminal psychologist Robert Hare is also the main man when it comes to spotting psychopathic personalities. Dr. Hare created the PCL-R, a test that can be used as a tool to determine whether someone is a psychopath, and it is considered to be the gold standard test across various disciplines. However, Hare expressly warns against nonprofessionals diagnosing those around them—so don't do that. *Just observe and feel smug at how clever you are.*

Hare laid out 20 key characteristics in relation to psychopathy. If a characteristic is spotted partially in a person, they get 1 point. If a characteristic applies to the person *fully*, they get 2 points. If a trait is not present at all, they are given—you've got it—no points. If an individual scores more than 30 points, they are, according to Hare, a psychopath. Interestingly, in the UK a score of 25 will get you over the psychopath line. What can we say, we just have lower standards when it comes to personality disorders *(and teeth, if you ask Americans).*

So let's take a look at the 20 characteristics, shall we?

❶ Glibness and superficial charm

❷ Grandiose sense of self-worth

❸ Pathological lying

❹ Conning/manipulative

❺ Lack of remorse or guilt

❻ Emotional shallowness/ a shallow affect

❼ Callousness and lack of empathy

❽ Failure to accept responsibility for actions

❾ A tendency toward boredom/ a need for stimulation

❿ A parasitic lifestyle

⑪ A lack of realistic long-term goals

⑫ Impulsivity

⑬ Irresponsibility

⑭ Poor behavioral control

⑮ Behavioral problems in early life

⑯ Juvenile delinquency

⑰ Criminal versatility

⑱ A history of "revocation of conditional release" (i.e., violating parole, skipping bail)

⑲ Multiple marriages/many short-term relationships

⑳ Promiscuous sexual behavior

We all know someone who displays some of these traits; maybe we even display a few ourselves. For example, Suruthi impulsively buys skin care products and silk hair turbans, whereas Hannah gets bored at the speed of light, and we've both had our fair share of short-term relationships. But each trait exists on a spectrum, and there's a threshold that needs to be met in terms of how damagingly impulsive you are, or just how lacking in empathy you are. If your behaviors fall within the parameters of what is generally acceptable and they don't negatively impact your life, they don't count. This is why assessment needs to be done via a clinician interview. Read our sidebar on Ted Bundy and his PCL-R test score to see why this checklist is still very subjective and open to interpretation.

TED BUNDY

Usually, you can't utter the word *psychopath* without hearing the name Ted Bundy being whispered on the wind. And this time is no different, but Bundy's PCL-R score is all over the bloody place. It is reported to be anywhere between the low 20s and a perfect score of 40. Lynne Awe and her paper, "Who Are They? The Psychopath and the Serial Killer Personality—Differences, Detection, and Diagnosis," peg him at 24. Whereas, in "Psychopathy and Gender of Serial Killers: A Comparison Using the PCL-R," Chasity Shalon Norris gives him a 33, the highest in her comparative study. And trusty Wikipedia will tell you Bundy scores an almost perfect 39, so you can make of that what you will . . .

Psycho Killer,
Qu'est-ce que c'est?

So far in this chapter we've talked about how psychopathy is predominantly genetic, but now the question is: Does having psychopathy *really* make you more likely to be a killer?

Well, the stats are immediately far more interesting than with the warrior gene. For example, studies estimate that around 1 percent of the general population are psychopaths, and that about 16 percent of incarcerated males and around 7 percent of incarcerated females are psychopaths—so that's *quite* an overrepresentation. But the issue is the latter figures include non-murderers and even nonviolent offenders, so let's consider another study to understand the extent to which *murder* and psychopathy are linked.

In 2018, the international study "Psychopathic Killers: A Meta-Analytic Review of the Psychopathy-Homicide Nexus" found that all the murderers in their sample had a higher tendency toward psychopathy than the average person, and that using the PCL-R checklist, just over a third of convicted murderers could be considered psychopaths.

The study also went a step further and found that the *more* violent and extreme the murder (if it involved sexual and sadistic elements, for instance), then the higher on average the psychopathy score of the killer. This isn't the only study to show this link; according to a study by psychiatrist Dr. Michael Stone—"Serial Sexual Homicide: Biological, Psychological, and Sociological Aspects"—a massive 86 percent of serial killers are psychopaths.

In multiple studies, a clear link has been shown between psychopathy and violent crime, particularly murder. We think it's fair to say that psychopathic traits—callousness, recklessness, impulsivity, a lack of empathy, and being driven by your own pleasure and self-interest—can lead to certain people committing horrific crimes. However, psychopathy on its own does not explain all the things that make a killer tick, as we will see over the course of this book.

"Curing" Psychopathy?

Is psychopathy curable? Short answer: no. Long answer: Also, kinda no ...

Hear us out, though, because this is a really important consideration. In the Bradley Waldroup case, we saw jurors' hesitation to convict a man of murder if his genetics had played a significant role in driving his behavior. *But* on the flip side, there are *many* more cases in which the prosecution will successfully argue that a killer who has a personality disorder, or is psychopathic, can't be cured or rehabilitated, so they should be locked up indefinitely. This doesn't strike us as fair, and we don't think that genetic conditions like this should play such a big role in sentencing either way (though obviously we're not talking about conditions that affect a person's intelligence, agency, or comprehension, which can of course influence culpability).

So how do we tackle this? Well, there is no magic fix for psychopathy, but some behavioral studies have found that people with psychopathic traits can be made "functionally successful." We'll talk about this in more detail in the next chapter when we discuss children who display signs of psychopathy, but for now we'll focus on the rehabilitation possibilities for psychopaths who have already offended.

Let's look mainly at the research of Dr. Kent Kiehl, neuroscientist at the University of New Mexico. Dr. Kiehl—after confirming his career-long suspicions that psychopathic brains are built differently from birth—decided to find out if that really meant that psychopathic people had no choice but to be bad. What he discovered was that while a carrot-and-stick approach works for most people, it doesn't work for psychopaths. Psychopaths generally don't care about consequences *(or sticks),* so punishment doesn't make them act "better." In fact, it usually makes them worse.

Psychopaths are six times more likely than other criminals to reoffend after they are released from prison, and no one, including Dr. Kiehl, thought there was any way around that. Indeed, psychopathy seemed utterly untreatable until the Mendota Juvenile Treatment Center (MJTC) in Wisconsin started a groundbreaking program they called the "decompression model."

This center for juvenile delinquents trialed a revolutionary approach to rehabilitation based on positive reinforcement rather than negative. Decompression is the opposite of punishment. Three hundred kids at MJTC had good behaviors positively reinforced by the staff at every possible juncture and were rewarded with candy bars and video games when they met targets. The study recorded that in the group of boys rehabilitated using the decompression model, recidivism was reduced by 34 percent.

On top of that, the young people who had been treated with positive reinforcement at MJTC were 50 percent less likely to later commit a violent crime, and none of them went on to kill people. Prior to their exposure to this model, almost all of the boys sent to MJTC were "deemed uncontrollable at other institutions," and most of them had at least 12 charges filed against them and high PCL-R scores (well, the baby version of the test given to people under 18). These results showed that the decompression model *significantly* improved behavior in juvenile boys who had been diagnosed as psychopaths. Which is, as Kiehl put it, "staggering."

More staggering than that, though, is the fact that those subjects of the study who did *not* receive the decompression treatment went on to commit 16 murders between them. These findings are hard to argue with, and it looks pretty likely that when it comes to psychopaths, early intervention and more carrot than stick are key.

CHILDHOOD AND ADOLESCENCE

Mommy Issues, Morbid Knights, and Murder Prodigies

IT FEELS LIKE A GLARINGLY OBVIOUS POINT TO MAKE THAT a killer's childhood has a massive impact on their future murder-y ambitions. But let's talk about it anyway, because it's fascinating—*and* there are still some surprises to be had and debunking to be done.

From birth to age five, a child's brain develops more than at *any* other time in life. So early brain development—and anything that may interfere with this, such as neglect, abuse, and trauma—can have an intense and lasting effect on a child's future, including, in some cases, the possibility of them growing up to be the next Ted Bundy. *(Well, minus the bell-bottoms and the unibrow, unless of course these things make a comeback. In a post-2020 world, anything could happen.)*

But it's not just early childhood that's important; what about the teenage years? Is there a more horrifying time in one's life than the transition to adolescence? The acne, the puberty, the crippling social pressure, the Dream Matte mousse foundation, and the fact that the teenage brain is actually *drawn* to danger and risky behavior. This can make even the most run-of-the-mill adolescence a time of impulsivity, low empathy, and stress, leading to such terrible decisions as playing chat roulette with strangers on the internet, giving oneself aggressive blonde cap highlights, and perhaps most disturbingly of all, thinking white pedal pushers are acceptable.

Now imagine the same hormonal changes and poor decision-making happening in an individual who is *already* genetically predisposed to psychopathy *and* who experienced an abusive childhood; we start to see the recipe for a killer emerge. But in these cases, how can one distinguish red flags indicating that perhaps something sinister is afoot from just normal teenage angst? And what, if anything, can or should be done about it? Most murderers don't kill until their late twenties or beyond, but is it possible to discern killers, especially serial killers, as children? And if somehow we could, *should* children be labeled and diagnosed if they appear to show a tendency toward violent, destructive, or psychopathic behavior? Could this prevent a child from growing up to be a killer, or would it simply create a self-fulfilling prophecy and a way in which society further disadvantages a child who has already had a rough start in life?

There is a *lot* to discuss when it comes to killers and their childhoods. In this chapter, we're going to examine different types of killers based on early childhood abuse and trauma, and whether labeling individuals who have psychopathic warning signs in childhood and adolescence is the right move.

Kids Don't Come with a "Factory Reset"

Now, before we jump into the impact of abuse on future behavior, it is important to stress that, of course, the vast majority of people who have suffered some form of trauma in their childhoods *do not* grow up to become violent, let alone killers.

And while not *all* killers are victims of abuse, most studies do agree that the majority of killers share a common backstory of past childhood trauma. For example, Heather Mitchell and Michael Aamodt's 2005 study, "The Incidence of Child Abuse in Serial Killers," showed that at least 26 percent of serial killers had experienced childhood sexual abuse, 36 percent had experienced physical abuse, and a whopping 50 percent had been psychologically abused as children.

The same report also found that serial killers were six times more likely to have been physically abused and nine times more likely to have been sexually abused than the general population.

Research shows what we already logically suspected: abusing a child most certainly increases the likelihood of that child growing up to be more violent. And before you're like, *well, duh,* as obvious as this point feels, the reasons for this link are multilayered and worth talking about.

Why does childhood abuse drive a killer? There are two reasons.

First, abuse may cause brain damage. And that damage can cause actual structural changes to the child's brain, which can lead to cognitive processing problems and lowered impulse control, two key traits often linked to killers. This brain damage can also be a result of an accidental head injury; killers like Fred West, Edmund Kemper, John Wayne Gacy, Richard Ramirez, Jerry Brudos, Gary Heidnik, and Ed Gein, to name just a few, all suffered serious head injuries as children or adolescents.

This kind of brain damage can, in some cases, induce psychopathy, and we have seen from the numerous studies we discussed in chapter 1 that the brain of a person with psychopathy is fundamentally different. Remember, it tends to show low levels of arousal in the prefrontal cortex, the part of the brain that is responsible for executive functions like planning, decision-making, and analyses of stimuli and self-control.

Studies have also found that those who go on to become psychopaths and repeat offenders often tend to struggle with processing verbal material; this is so vital because processing verbal material is absolutely crucial in our ability to understand social rules. Essentially, the brain of a psychopathic killer is out of balance because the logical, rational part of the brain isn't functioning; the brakes of the brain aren't working. The person knows the difference between right and wrong, but they struggle to stop and think before they act. The second reason abuse may forge one's path to murder is that the abuse may lead to the development of massive unresolved trauma. For some individuals, this trauma could drive them to engage in traumatic reenactment later in life.

What Is Traumatic Reenactment?

Traumatic reenactment is defined as "lingering behavioral enactment and automatic repetition of the past." Still not sure what that means? Don't worry, you're about to; trust us, by the end of this book everyone you know will be totally exhausted by how clever you are. *(You'll lose friends, but who needs those when you have serial killer brain pattern knowledge?)*

In his book *Serial Killers*, psychologist Joel Norris describes the psychological phases that serial killers experience, from the "aura phase" to the "depression phase." Norris's theory links closely to the concept of traumatic reenactment, because as he points out, the "murder phase" becomes a *ritual reenactment* of past trauma and abuse from the killer's childhood.

Essentially what's happening is that the killer is *recreating* their own childhood trauma, but this time instead of *them* being the victim, they have reversed the roles. In a (horrendously destructive) way, this is a killer with a huge unresolved trauma from their childhood trying to deal with their issues. By victimizing someone else, they are attempting to take back control and power and gain mastery over the trauma they suffered.

Particularly with serial killers, when you combine structural brain issues and abuse, *and* top it off with a genetic predisposition to psychopathy—*boom*; you could have on your hands a person broken by their childhood trauma, filled with rage, shame, and a need to dominate. Now couple this with lower impulse control. When asked during an interview with blogger Eric Barker what makes a serial killer, former New York State prosecutor, former FBI profiler, and now fellow true crime podcaster Jim Clemente said, "It's a mix of bio, psycho, and social. The biology is your genetics, what you're born with. Your psychology and your personality; you have a certain amount of it when you're born, but you actually participate in the development of that throughout your entire life. And then there are the events that happen in your life, your socialization. So the way I like to say it is: your genetics load the gun, your personality aims it, and the events in your life pull the trigger."

And while this does offer a well-rounded answer to a question that has plagued humanity for decades, there is a deeper dive we can take on why there are so many *different types* of serial killer. Not only is a horrific childhood more likely to set someone on the path to becoming a killer, but also the specific *type* of abuse endured may actually explain the type of killer that they go on to become.

Killers can be broken down into four types: thrill killers, mission-oriented killers, power killers, and visionary killers.

Going in for the Kill: Thrill Killers

These killers derive their satisfaction from the *process* of a murder rather than the act of the kill itself; they are driven by sheer excitement and adrenaline. This type of killer may taunt the police with phone calls and notes because it adds an extra layer of excitement for them. Thrill killers are possibly the hardest to catch because they don't really have a typical profile like some other types; generally speaking, they tend to be male and younger in age, but that's about it. The main factor that unites thrill killers is a feeling of inadequacy or being marginalized in ordinary life. (Though as we'll discover, when it comes to killers, that doesn't narrow it down a whole hell of a lot.)

If you're trying to wrap your head around a thrill killer, think of the 2002 Sandra Bullock film *Murder by Numbers*. If you haven't seen that little gem *(what's wrong with you?)*, then let's consider the classic example of a couple of thrill killers: Nathan Leopold and Richard Loeb. Leopold and Loeb were a pair of wealthy, highly intelligent students who seemed to have it all, but they also seem to have been relentlessly bored with life, and so they decided to kidnap and murder a 14-year-old boy named Robert "Bobby" Franks. The pair's only motivation behind this killing was to see if they could get away with the "perfect crime." For them, the planning, the buildup, and the chance to see if they could outsmart authorities offered the biggest payoff, rather than the actual murder itself.

Above the Law: Mission-Oriented Killers

These killers believe, or *claim* to believe, that they have a greater purpose on earth—a higher calling—and that through their murderous actions, they are actually making the world a better place. Most killers tend to develop their own code of ethics; after all, no one is a monster in their own story *(that's why your ex-boyfriend still has friends)*. But mission-oriented killers take it to the next level. They want to bring the rest of the world in line with their own personal morals and standards, and so they usually target groups or individuals that they deem undesirable. These killers are rarely very original though, and most tend to victimize sex workers or members of the LGBTQ community, then justify their actions by stating that it is their duty to purge the world of [insert group]. These killers will rationalize that their victims deserved to die because they were a scourge on this earth, morally inferior, and blasphemous. And so, the notion that they are killing for a greater good allows them an escape, a moral get out of jail free card.

The important thing to remember here, though, is that we aren't talking about killers who are being pushed by voices or visions to kill (that's another type of killer); mission-oriented killers have taken it upon themselves to act. We also know that most are not solely motivated by their "mission"; some just use it as an excuse.

Take, for example, Gary Ridgway (a.k.a. the Green River Killer). For a long time Ridgway was America's most deadly convicted serial killer. He confessed to having murdered up to 80 women, mainly sex workers, in and around Washington state in the 1980s and 1990s. He claimed, "I wanted to kill as many women as I thought were prostitutes as I possibly could, because I hated them."

Ridgway said that these sex workers were "unclean" and had to die. However, he raped these women before killing them, a fact which hardly supports the warped mission he claimed he wanted to fulfill, and shows him for what most killers like him truly are. They conflate their actions with a perceived higher moral cause when, really, they tend to just be driven by animalistic, sexual depravity and a need to dominate. But of course admitting their true reasons, even to themselves, would undermine their whole holier than thou spiel.

Deliberate Dominance: Power Killers

These killers, as the name suggests, seek above all else power, control, and domination of their victims. They enjoy humiliating and torturing their "prey" and tend to gain sexual pleasure from the pain and suffering of their captives. Ted Bundy is the perfect example of a power killer—he would rape his victims as he killed them, but also hide their bodies and return to the corpses later to "interfere" with them. This is because necrophilia—although the victim is already dead—still allows the killer to gain *absolute* control and dominance. Power killers are probably the most common type of serial killer, and even if at first it seems that another category is a better fit, almost all male serial killers will show traits consistent with being a power killer.

The Voice of God: Visionary Killers

And last but certainly not least, let's talk about visionary killers. These killers suffer from some sort of psychosis that makes them prone to delusions and hallucinations. These visions often lead the killer to feel compelled, or even ordered, to kill. The most common apparitions that visit such killers are religious in nature, featuring God or the devil. This is an interesting type of killer because it is exceedingly rare in reality, but so hyped by Hollywood that it has become an archetypal killer we expect to constantly come across. It is also fascinating, because it can be very difficult to prove whether someone is truly hearing voices and having hallucinations driving them to kill, or whether they are just malingering.

David Berkowitz (a.k.a. Son of Sam) is a perfect example of the latter. He terrorized New York during the summer of 1976, killing six people and wounding seven others in a series of shootings across the city. When he was eventually caught, he claimed to have been ordered to kill by his neighbor "Sam" who passed messages to him through his dog. Berkowitz claimed that the dog was possessed by the devil and that it spoke to him in demonic voices, telling him to kill. But despite this story, Berkowitz was found mentally competent to stand trial, found guilty, and sentenced to life in prison. Much to absolutely no one's surprise, Berkowitz later admitted that the whispering devil dog story was totally made up. Now this isn't to say that *no* killer is driven by these kinds of voices—they certainly can be. But we're going to leave aside visionary killers for now and come back to them in the next chapter.

For the rest of the killers, just to simplify things, we're going to group them another way, into three specific categories based on their motivations and behavior: power, lust, and anger.

* **Power killers** are those who derive pleasure from having complete control over their victims.

* **Lust killers (sexually motivated thrill killers)** are motivated to kill for their own sexual gratification.

* **Anger killers** are those who kill because of feelings of anger or betrayal.

So while we know that childhood abuse definitely influences a killer, an interesting question to consider is, what actually forms their varying motivations?

The February study "A Behavior Sequence Analysis of Serial Killers' Lives: From Childhood Abuse to Methods of Murder" starts to unravel this link between types of childhood abuse and the resulting types of killer and behaviors. The authors examined the histories of 233 male serial killers, and found that whether the killer had experienced sexual, physical, or psychological abuse as a child—or some combination of the three—actually determined their different motivations to kill, and presented in *distinct* behaviors and MOs (*modus operandi,* i.e., the particular way in which a killer carries out their acts). Like most of us would, the researchers predicted that killers who had experienced childhood sexual abuse would predominantly be lust killers. But interestingly, while the study did find a clear link between the type of abuse and the later typology of the serial killer, it discovered that killers who were abused sexually were most likely to become *power* killers, not lust killers. The researchers also found that lust killers were most frequently formed when a killer had suffered psychological abuse, or a combination of all three types of abuse (psychological, physical, and sexual) as a child, rather than sexual abuse alone.

The results also showed that aspects of the way killers carried out their murders could be linked to their childhood abuse experiences. It appears from this study that killers who were physically abused as children were more likely to demonstrate "overkill" of their victims, using unnecessarily excessive force to complete the kill. But the study found that the most sadistic and brutal killings (those involving torture and mutilation) were carried out by those who had been sexually and/or psychologically abused in early childhood.

The overkill we see with killers, particularly male ones, who were physically abused calls to mind the findings of the classic Bobo doll experiment. In 1961, psychologist Albert Bandura conducted an experiment that determined that children can learn aggressive social behaviors through observation and imitation. During the experiment, a team of researchers physically and verbally abused an inflatable doll in front of some small children. The children, mainly the boys, later imitated the aggressive behavior and attacked the doll in the same way they had seen.

Going back to the serial killers study—why is it that the ones who were sexually abused went on to most often become power killers, who kill quickly, rather than lust killers as one might expect? One theory is that those killers who experienced sexual abuse suffer from shame and deep levels of anger and self-blame, leading them to lash out and kill their victims quickly. They may also be more likely to feel guilt or remorse afterward, and therefore their murders may be less likely to show evidence of overkill or mutilation.

While these studies are fascinating, every killer's story is different and the information we are working with is imperfect. To start with, usually the main way a killer's pre-capture life, especially their childhood, is documented is through interviews with the murderer themselves. So we have to consider how much we can rely on self-reported tales.

Serial killers don't make for the most reliable of narrators, for obvious reasons. Some will hide their early abuse because they fear the shame. Those who are deeply insecure, particularly about, say, their masculinity, could never allow themselves to share something that would make them so vulnerable; it would be a sign of weakness. On the flip side, we also have the killers who use their abusive childhoods as an excuse to absolve themselves of their horrific actions, thereby refusing to take accountability or responsibility for what they have done.

As we discussed in chapter 1, when a baby is born, they come into the world a bundle of joy and with bundles of genetic predisposition; the genetic dice have already been rolled. What happens next—the lottery of the parenting they receive, the experiences they have, and the environment they grow up in—is, just like with genetics, totally out of baby's control, but just as vital.

Let's now put these theories into context. We'll explore a lesser-known killer who had a pretty shocking childhood, and discuss the likely impact that neglect, abuse, family dysfunction, damaging parents, and trauma had on his descent into depravity.

Jurgen Bartsch
(the Murderous Child "Prodigy")

On November 6, 1946, in Essen, West Germany, a young unwed mother named Anna Sadrozinski had a baby boy she named Karl. Tragically, however, Anna died soon after little Karl was born. He was left in the hospital to be looked after by the busy nurses until he was later moved to an orphanage.

For the first 11 months of his life, Karl was given perfectly adequate shelter and protection, but no personal love or affection. Almost immediately, therefore, we see with baby Karl a storm on the horizon. So before we delve into his story, let's look at how this early experience may have contributed to his later behavior.

The first year of a baby's life is absolutely vital in terms of emotional, psychological, and linguistic development, and the impact of early neglect, or even indifference, on a child can be monumental. Let's think of a baby's brain and the seeds of neural pathways that exist. If the baby is shown love and attention, their brain will blossom and the pathways will grow. But in the brain of a neglected baby, fewer connections are built. Once the window of opportunity closes for some of these pathways to be formed, the psychological and linguistic deficits created can be extremely difficult, and in some cases impossible, to rectify later in life.

As shown by a 2020 study in *Current Psychology*, a child's ability to express emotions may also be shaped during this time. As we saw in chapter 1, many people who are diagnosed with antisocial personality disorder, or who show psychopathic traits, tend to have a shallow or blunted affect. They have trouble communicating their emotions and appear to have less animated facial or vocal expressions. One common psychopathic trait is an inability to recognize emotion in others; this and the shallow affect may, in some cases, stem from indifference that the baby experienced from its parents. This is because when a caregiver doesn't respond to a baby with positive and expressive reactions, it can cause a baby's emotions (and expression of their emotions) to flatline.

Which comes first? Is it the child ("chicken") with psychopathic traits—such as being callous and unemotional, perhaps crying constantly and never smiling—making it harder for parents to show warm parenting?

Or the neglectful parents ("egg") who shape a troubled child through their disdain and abuse?

There isn't a really clear-cut answer to this, but something that is strongly backed up by the research is the theory of attachment and the role it plays in the development of one's personality. Because aside from emotional and psychological milestones that need to be met, there are also key stages of bonding between baby and caregivers that need to occur during this time. And again, if the opportunity is missed, the effects can be lifelong and devastating. That first year in particular is crucial to the proper development of the adult personality, because it's during this time that children start to develop a sense of self and feelings of remorse, empathy, and affection. If a baby doesn't get enough emotional attention or physical touch in those early days, it can lead to the development of substantial personality issues in the future.

We don't need to delve into the world of serial killers—or even humans—to understand the importance of warmth, affection, and love. In the 1950s, American psychologist Harry Harlow conducted his now-famous monkey experiment. Basically, he gave baby monkeys the option of a mother monkey figure made from a wire frame, holding a milk bottle, or a soft and furry monkey mother without a milk bottle. Every single baby monkey in the experiment chose the soft fake monkey mommy to cuddle with at the expense of food. They were willing to go hungry to get the closest thing they could to affection. However, the monkeys that went through this experiment as babies never managed to integrate with other monkeys and form social bonds in later life, because although instinctively they made the choice to pick "affection" from the furry monkey mommy, they didn't actually get the nurturing and love they needed from these fake mommies. These monkeys spent the rest of their lives confused, afraid, and isolated.

And if that's not enough eye-opening misery for you, don't worry—there's more to come.

"Slaughterhouses of the Souls"

For a horribly sad mass example of the devastating impact of a lack of healthy emotional bonding in childhood, we need to head to Romania. In 1966, then dictator Nicolae Ceausescu banned abortion and any form of contraceptive in order to keep the country's population from plummeting after World War II. But, predictably, forcing people to have children they aren't willing or able to look after led to thousands and thousands of children ending up in orphanages across Romania.

It is estimated that around 170,000 Romanian children were abandoned in such institutions, which became known as "child gulags" or "the slaughterhouses of the souls." At the end of 1989 the communist dictatorship finally fell, and Romania's plight would be one of such horror that it would go on to be dubbed "the shame of the nation."

It was in 1990 that the outside world discovered the nightmarish truth of what was really going on. The story broke in a brutally visual way: ABC's *20/20* aired a stomach-turning exposé that showed hundreds of skeletal children living in unspeakable conditions. The buildings were dark, freezing, and overcrowded; tiny, dirty children sat muttering and rocking back and forth alone in cribs and cages. The floors were covered in feces and urine and it was clear that most of the children were suffering from untreated medical conditions. Some of the "children" were later discovered to be in their twenties and were no bigger than three feet tall.

In 2000, Harvard pediatric neuroscientist Charles Nelson led the Bucharest Early Intervention Project. Researchers worked with 136 children, aged between six months to two and a half years, from these Romanian orphanages to assess the quality of the attachment relationships between the children and their caregivers or parents. In the control group (made up of children from the local community) 100 percent of the children had a fully developed attachment relationship with their mother. Only 3 percent of the institutionalized kids had this. Even worse, 13 percent of the institutionalized children were deemed "unclassified," meaning they showed no attachment behaviors at all. This was unbelievable to the researchers, because the theory prior to this experiment had been that a child would attach to even the most abusive of adults, like the baby monkey clinging to the fake monkey mommy that shows it no love. No one had ever considered that there could be children who simply didn't form attachments.

This revealed that seeking comfort for distress is a *learned* behavior (another point for team "nurture"). These children had grown up with no idea that an adult could make them feel better. This discovery, alongside Harlow's experiments, showed that a strong emotional bond with one's parents or caregivers—or what psychologists call "secure attachment"—is crucial to good health and flourishing later in life. Not forming a healthy emotional bond was also proven to cause an extremely wide range of issues; these children developed autistic-like behaviors, like repetitively rocking or banging their heads. They were also affected physically: their head circumferences were significantly smaller than average, they had severely weakened immune systems, and they struggled to gain weight.

Once again, these are very extreme examples and most people who have poor parental relationships or attachment disorders do not go on to become violent in any way, much less killers. But as British psychiatrist and father of attachment theory John Bowlby put it, there is no denying that attachment is an emotional bond that affects behavior "from the cradle to the grave." Some sociologists and psychologists now actually consider psychopathic or sociopathic behavior to be the brain's defense mechanism when dealing with a neglectful childhood or early trauma.

So, given that we now know early infant bonding is absolutely vital to personality development, it will come as no surprise that a common experience shared by some serial killers, such as David Berkowitz, Joel Rifkin, and Kenneth Bianchi, is that they were adopted during this vital period of their lives. Now, we have to remember that that was just one of many factors. Obviously, it's certainly not the case that all adoptees have serious personality issues; many, many people are adopted into loving homes and go on to live healthy lives. What we can say is that if these men had experienced warm parenting right from the very start and through-out their childhoods, it's possible that their violent behavior might never have expressed itself.

Let's get back to Germany and baby Karl. As he was about to turn one, Karl was adopted by a couple—a butcher named Gerhard Bartsch and his wife Gertrud. They renamed the baby boy Jurgen and took him home. As discussed, the first 12 months of a person's life are vital. Although he was adopted relatively early, it's clear Jurgen hadn't received the right amount of love, affection, or attention by age one. And if anyone thought that being adopted was the start of an amazing new life for baby Jurgen, they would be very wrong indeed. Life post-adoption would be anything but easy for him. Jurgen's new father paid him absolutely no attention—except, that is, when he was beating little Jurgen on the floor of his abattoir. He would also often lock Jurgen up overnight in his underground cellar for even the most minor misbehavior.

Jurgen's mother, on the other hand, seems to have been incredibly overbearing. Paul Moor, the author of the book *Jürgen Bartsch: Selbstbild-*

nis eines Kindermörders, described Jurgen's mother as "completely over-protective and emotionally withdrawn," which is bad enough, but then to top it off it appears that Gertrud was also far too hands on with her son. She was obsessed with cleanliness and became convinced that if Jurgen ever played with the other children he would become "dirty." Her rather unconventional remedy for this was to personally bathe Jurgen with her own two hands, even when he was no longer a small child. She did this until he was arrested for a series of horrific murders at the age of 19.

Mommy Issues

At this point, Jurgen Bartsch is starting to rack up some serious points on the old serial killer bingo sheet, because another common characteristic among serial killers, as some of us know, is their dysfunctional relationships with their mothers. In the book *Whoever Fights Monsters,* former FBI agent Robert Ressler concludes: "Without exception the relationship of the interviewed serial murderers to their mother was determined by coolness, distance, lack of love, and neglect. They hardly experienced emotional warmth or body contact." And no, being washed by your mom until you're 19 doesn't count as decent body contact.

In her 2016 documentary series *Murderers and Their Mothers,* Dr. Elizabeth Yardley, professor of criminology and director of Birmingham City University's Centre for Applied Criminology, examines the complex nature of the killer-mother relationship. She, like most other researchers, finds that the mother's influence in the making of a murderer cannot be overstated. *But why?* I hear you scream. *Isn't laying the blame at the feet of their mothers just more sexist bullshit?* Well, unfortunately, our society is deeply engendered whether we like it or not, and we expect mothers to be the safety net, emotionally speaking. If we were to look at killer after killer and examine their relationship with their mother, we'd find to varying degrees—either through outright abuse, their willingness to ignore the red flags in front of them, or their indifference—mothers begin to shape these killers right from the start.

During his early childhood, Jurgen Bartsch was already dealing with some pretty hefty trauma being piled on him at home. And as if this regular psychological and physical abuse weren't enough, things were about to get a whole lot worse.

At the age of 12, Bartsch was sent off to everyone's favorite God-sponsored abuse pit—a Catholic boarding school. And in a thoroughly on-brand scenario, some pretty dark shit went on there. When Bartsch was just 12, he was stricken with polio; during a particularly bad night in bed, writhing from a raging fever, the school's choir leader Father Pütlitz raped him. The abuse went on for years and Pütlitz was quite the entertainer; he went so far as to lace his abuse of Bartsch with sadistic stories of a medieval knight who killed little boys (see sidebar).

GILLES DE RAIS: THE SATANIC CHILD-KILLING KNIGHT

Obviously, once we read about a serial-killing knight, we had to look it up to see if it was real, or if it was just from the dark recesses of Pütlitz's mind. As it turns out, it was very real indeed.

Baron de Rais was a knight and Lord from Brittany, Anjou, and Poitou (let's just call it France).

He was a big deal in King Charles VII of France's army and also mates with good old flame-fighting warrior of God Joan of Arc. But his CV doesn't end there, oh no. Rais was like an olden-timey QAnon conspiracy theorist's wet dream; he was massively into alchemy, demon summoning, and child murder. He was convinced that if he could just find and read the right old books and manage to get his hands on enough candles and incense, he'd be able to summon a demon, no matter what it cost him. So like a nineties teenager at a Halloween sleepover, Rais started to dabble in the occult and tried to summon a demon named Barron.

After three unsuccessful attempts, and no demon manifesting itself, Rais decided that the ritual was lacking a little *je ne sais quoi* in the shape of child body parts. So off he went, and kicking off in the spring of 1432, he abducted, sodomized, and murdered anywhere between 100 to 600 young boys. Although he was finally caught and put to death in October 1440, Gilles de Rais has forever marked his place in popular culture, as he was the main inspiration for the folktale of Bluebeard.

Just three years later in 1962, at age 15, Jurgen Bartsch would kill his first victim, eight-year-old Klaus Jung. He convinced Jung to follow him into an abandoned air-raid shelter and then forced Jung to strip before he raped and killed him.

This in itself is highly unusual; often with serial killers there first is a buildup of escalating crimes. Very few go straight to rape and murder at the age of 15. Typically, they have a long rap sheet of misdemeanors, including petty crimes, theft, and Peeping Tom–like behavior, well into their late teens and early twenties. Although their fantasies of dominance, control, and power usually begin to kick in in childhood and their early teens, the average serial killer doesn't typically commit their first murder until their mid to late twenties.

A lot of serial killers, particularly power and lust killers, get started as Peeping Toms as a way to dip their toes into the dirty pool of boundary-violation and get their first taste of dominance over others. Some of the most notorious and prolific serial killers, such as Joseph DeAngelo (a.k.a. the Golden State Killer), Dennis Rader (a.k.a. BTK), and Ted Bundy, all started off as Peeping Toms. Jurgen Bartsch is a rare serial murderer in that he skipped all of this and went straight for the kill. He was having violent fantasies as a child and he acted on them immediately.

Bartsch's second victim was 13-year-old Peter Fuchs in 1965. As you can see, Bartsch waited three years between his first two kills, which is typical of serial killers. Often they have cooling-off periods between kills that get shorter and shorter as the killer needs more of a thrill more frequently to sustain their appetite. But once again Bartsch was a fast mover—he escalated greatly and within the next two years he had killed two more boys: 12-year-old Ulrich Kahlweiss and 12-year-old Manfred Grassman.

Usually, a serial killer's MO and behavior evolve over time as they learn what they like, work to refine their "art," and increase their criminal sophistication to evade capture. But Bartsch went so hard and fast there was very little deviation between his kills. As outlined in his 2005 study "Two Homosexual Pedophile Sadistic Serial Killers," Mark Benecke explains that all of Jurgen Bartsch's kills, generally speaking, were incredibly similar: he would lure the boys somewhere secluded, rape them, and usually kill them by strangulation. Afterward, Bartsch would dismember the boys' bodies; he would decapitate them, chop them up, and remove all of their innards. He removed the boys' eyes, castrated them, and removed chunks of flesh such as the thighs and buttocks. He would then bury the remains in a tunnel a few miles outside of the town. He did all this between the ages of just 15 and 19. His fifth would-be victim—15-year-old Peter Frese—managed to escape by using a candle to burn through the ropes that were binding him. He went straight to the police and Jurgen Bartsch was caught.

It is morbidly fascinating how many children Bartsch was able to kill at such a young age. It is also believed that he made at least another one hundred unsuccessful murder attempts before being apprehended. As we've highlighted, to see such serial offenses in someone so young is highly unusual, but Bartsch also stands out in another way because he straddled the line between being a process killer *and* a product killer. His testimony at trial revealed that he was quite the hybrid. Let's take a look at the differences:

* A **process killer** is a killer who enjoys the buildup to a kill and the actual kill itself. They want to hear their victim scream and watch the life drain from their victim's body. These killers will usually prolong the killing process as long as possible and engage in torture and captivity. They want their victims to suffer because that's what turns them on. Sexual sadist Dennis Rader (a.k.a. BTK, for Bind, Torture, Kill) is the perfect example of a process killer.

* A **product killer**, on the other hand, doesn't get pleasure from the actual kill; they just want the body and the remains *after* the murder is complete. The murder is a necessary hurdle to cross in order to get what they really want—a dead body. Jeffrey Dahmer is a classic example of a product killer; he killed to get what he wanted—a sex zombie. The kill itself didn't give him pleasure; it was the body he got to possess afterward that satisfied him.

Bartsch kind of falls into both camps. According to reports, at trial he talked openly about his fantasies; he emphasized that he only reached sexual climax while masturbating and cutting the flesh of his victims after their death. But Bartsch also stated that he wanted to skin a live child with soft skin, little hair, and a "non-aggressive mood." He claimed that this particular goal was not reached because the children had always died too fast. However, this didn't really stand in his way as he carried on regardless and dismembered the children's bodies and ejaculated onto their flesh. As you can see, Bartsch was very candid. The only part of his behavior that he would not openly comment on was if he had eaten any of the human meat. When asked, he would only say that he had "touched it with his lips." *(Hmmmm.)*

We know Bartsch's childhood and adolescence were filled with abuse, indifference, and sexual violence. This, possibly coupled with that first year he spent deprived of affection in an orphanage, as well as his own genetic predisposition toward violence, created a killer who was so filled with violent fantasies and rage that he didn't even wait until adulthood to strike. He didn't bother with slowly pushing boundaries. Jurgen Bartsch pounced as soon as he was able to and wouldn't have stopped until he was caught.

We have spent the majority of this chapter so far looking at how childhood abuse can form a killer, and we said at the start most serial killers had pretty fucked up childhoods. But did you know that recent studies show that more than a third of killers don't report any abuse or trauma from their younger days? Dennis Rader is a perfect example. A sexually sadistic serial killer, he had a (verifiably) perfectly ordinary childhood. So since there are killers that seem to be "natural born killers," the question becomes: Could anything be done in childhood to prevent one from heading down a murder-y path?

To explore this idea, let's consider the work of psychologist John Marshall. Dr. Marshall has spent more than two decades working with psychopaths, and in 2019 he put together a report on Aaron Campbell, a Scottish teenager who brutally killed a six-year-old girl, Alesha MacPhail. In his analysis, Dr. Marshall raised some important points that received their fair share of backlash. In a controversial article he penned in *The Scotsman* that same year, he said that he believed some social workers are in denial about child psychopaths, and that the children's services system in the UK clings far too closely to the idea that almost everything negative we see in a child who offends must be linked to some past trauma.

In his report on Campbell, a boy who had been showing worrying signs for a long time, Marshall writes: "No one becomes a psychopath on their sixteenth birthday. Psychopathic traits start in very early childhood, have predictable pathways, and yet we do not assess children for this neurodevelopmental problem. At the age of 16, such traits are already entrenched and chronic so it is time for policy to catch up with research, given the enormous social costs of psychopathy. We have to deal with psychopathy trajectories in childhood head-on now to divert budding psychopaths."

As we saw in chapter 1, this is highly accurate, because psychopathy is a congenital condition. So while of course not all psychopaths will go on to commit horrific crimes, they are at greater risk of becoming violent offenders, whether they experience trauma and abuse or not. However, as you can imagine, even in the wake of a young girl's murder these words were met with skepticism. The notion that by age 16, psychopathic traits are so deeply ingrained that, for all intents and purposes, that child could end up a lost cause hit hard. Dr. Marshall's main point in his report was that early identification is key, because multiple studies have shown that warm parenting can make a huge difference for children with psychopathic traits—but it has to happen early. The questions then are: How do you identify such traits in young children? And when would you label such children? And with what?

In most countries, professionals aren't allowed to diagnose antisocial personality disorder in someone under the age of 18. But if it can't be labeled, then how can it be treated effectively—especially when, according to Dr. Marshall, early intervention is key?

Professionals who advocate against the early labeling of children with terms like "psychopathic traits" or "pre-psychopaths" are worried about the stigma it may cause. Another problem is that almost all children exhibit some degree of antisocial behavior sometimes. They can be hostile, disobedient, and verbally and physically abusive. But what happens when these behaviors clearly cross a line? We spoke with a couple who reached out to us after listening to our podcast for years. Cassie and Mike have a teenage son, Arthur, who exhibits serious behavioral issues, such as violence against others, animal abuse, a lack of remorse, and callous, unemotional traits.

Arthur's behavior has followed a troubling trajectory throughout his childhood. He threw a neighbor's kittens against a wall, he would catch and kill rats for fun, and he once sent a video to his mom of him smashing live crabs with a screwdriver while laughing. From an early age, his behavior began to spiral—Arthur faced being expelled from school at just age four, but this didn't rein in his behavior. By age 10, Arthur had taken a knife into school with the intention of attacking another pupil. At age 12, he was inappropriately touching other children at school and eventually sexually assaulted another student. Arthur wasn't any better at home. He would stand silently in his parents' bedroom doorway at night and watch them sleep. Arthur also began to exhibit inappropriate behavior toward his younger sister and his mother. He started to compulsively watch hardcore pornography, he tried to drown his sister, and he even began making strange videos, almost like a manifesto.

Eventually, Arthur was placed in a children's care home, where he remains today at age 14. He regularly threatens and assaults staff emotionally, physically, and sexually; he even once attempted to induce an anaphylactic reaction in one of the caregivers after learning about her life-threatening allergy. Arthur runs away at any opportunity and is completely resistant to therapy. He says to his psychiatrist that in sessions he just tells him what he knows he wants to hear. Arthur shows no remorse, has no empathy, accepts no responsibility, and believes that everyone else is in the wrong for not letting him do as he wants.

Arthur is clearly displaying incredibly worrying signs and has almost since birth, but he cannot be diagnosed with antisocial personality disorder until he is at least 18—right around the time that he will be released from the children's home to integrate into society. Now don't get us wrong—exhibiting a conduct disorder and limited pro-social emotions in childhood isn't a definite path to a life of violence, but it does put that child at a greater risk of developing adult psychopathy and getting into trouble with the law in the future.

The Sorrow of the Psychopathic Child

So, what has Arthur been diagnosed with? The interesting thing is that many children like Arthur, who at a young age show conduct disorder and psychopathic traits, are generally diagnosed with and being treated for ADHD (attention deficit hyperactivity disorder), because they can't be diagnosed with ASPD. But in some cases, when for example the true cause of the behavioral issues is psychopathy or ASPD, this could be tremendously detrimental, because although these children will usually present as overactive, ironically they have the underactive brain of a psychopath, making ADHD medication the opposite of what they may need.

As we discussed in chapter 1, the brains of psychopaths are different. The prefrontal cortex is almost completely switched off and it shows very low levels of arousal to stimuli. These children who perhaps have psychopathic or non-pro-social traits have a severe inability to concentrate and so they fall behind in school; this is *not* an indicator of low intelligence, but as they fall behind their peers, they develop a low self-image. Unfortunately, this breeds frustration and further pushes the child to defy authority.

The growing negative self-perception then leads these children to do things that will give them immediate gratification. Thanks also to their less active prefrontal cortexes, these children seek excitement and stimulation from more and more extreme behavior in order to get their brain arousal levels to reach "normal." They will act on impulse, usually in a destructive and not-so–socially acceptable way. This kind of behavior will cause other children to become cautious of them and distance themselves, but the child with psychopathic traits will usually struggle to recognize emotions in others' faces, again hampering their ability to form a bond or to correct their behavior. This rejection compounds the child's negative perception of themselves and increases their feelings of isolation. The loneliness, coupled with a lack of normal social or academic achievement, plus the thrill-seeking behavior they use to light up their underactive brains, often culminates in criminal behavior.

If we did screen children for psychopathy early, would treatment work? We discussed in chapter 1 how psychopaths who have *already* committed a violent crime can be rehabilitated more effectively, but what about a *child* displaying psychopathic tendencies? Well, the evidence shows that treatment—in the shape of specific kinds of therapy and medication—can work, and the earlier it starts the better. But let's be clear, it's not so much a cure as it is an adjustment. A child doesn't have to grow up to become an active psychopath if they can learn to adjust to society and to control their urges. The psychopathy itself can't be eradicated, but the child can be made "functionally successful." Before you grimace that maybe this all sounds a bit *Clockwork Orange*-y, think about it: The psychopath is not happy or leading a fulfilling life—leave aside whether they are societally "good" or not. Treatment can help them manage their condition, and the byproduct is that they can go on to become a more productive (and less potentially dangerous) member of society.

The problem is that most children like this will not get the support or treatment they need, even though treatment at an early stage has been shown to be far, far, far cheaper for society than the impact if they do go on to offend in the future. Some studies, as assessed in the 1995 documentary *The Dangerous Few,* estimate that treatment would be about 1/1000th of the cost of incarceration as an adult, and that doesn't even take into account the lives that could have been saved.

There is no clear-cut solution to any of this, but we think that as a society we should definitely have more open conversations like the one that Dr. Marshall is proposing. But we also understand why this topic makes people uncomfortable and why any truly definitive action could be very difficult in practice.

INSANITY

Cacodemonomania, Culpability, and Christ-themed EDM

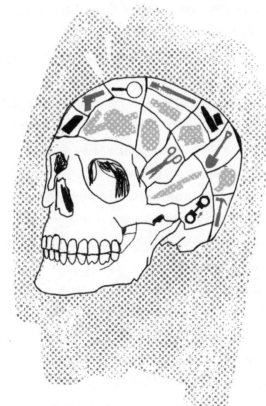

WHEN PEOPLE HEAR ABOUT HORRIFIC MURDERS, THEY almost automatically jump to say that the killer must have been *insane*. It's easy to understand why. But what does that actually *mean*?

Do they think that all murderers must have had a mental illness that made them kill? If so, that's not really the story statistics tell. Study after study on people who have committed violent crimes shows that the majority of killers exhibit no evidence of severe mental disorders. Dr. Michael Stone, a forensic psychiatrist at Columbia University, has collated a detailed database of mass killers dating back one hundred years. In 2017, he concluded that about 65 percent of them did not have a diagnosable mental disorder. According to Dr. Stone, the *majority* of the killers are angry, and they act on a deep sense of injustice that built up over time. They are *not* mentally ill.

Yet the notion that mental illness and criminality, especially murder, are inextricably linked is pervasive. We've even colloquially adopted a lot of clinical terminology, but unsurprisingly these words are often thrown around completely incorrectly. How often have you heard a person call someone else a psycho? Or heard the term *schitzo* being bandied around? The person doing the name calling here is probably referring to a person who is constantly changing their behavior or their temperament and is perhaps prone to mood swings.

According to the *DSM-5*, which is currently the key diagnostic tool used by mental health professionals, these wouldn't be anywhere near the symptoms of someone with schizophrenia. What they probably mean is dissociative identity disorder—formerly known as multiple personality disorder—yet symptom-wise they'd still be wrong anyway.

These misuses of clinical terminology highlight the continued stigma of mental illness, so it's important to say straight off the bat that people who suffer from mental illness are much more likely to be victims of crime than perpetrators of it. And people with untreated severe mental disorders are much more likely to be a danger to themselves, not others. The vilification of mental illness when it's presented as the sole reason why killers kill is at best overly simplistic, and at worst ignorant and dangerous.

A lot of the bias and misunderstanding around the issues of insanity is—in our opinion—largely due to the fact that we are absolutely inundated with TV shows, movies, and books that are obsessed with the concept of "the insanity defense," or "not guilty by reason of insanity." In reality, this highly contentious defense is used in the US less than 1 percent of the time! And it's only successful in a quarter of that 1 percent of cases. It is an exceedingly rare defense, and it's rarer still that it works, because there is an incredibly high bar to meet at trial.

So, because there is a huge amount of misinformation out there about what insanity truly is (for example the fact that it is not a clinical term, but actually a legal and cultural one)—we're going to have to be on top of our game this chapter to keep up with the tangled web of definitions and legal standards—let's go over the basics. Firstly, even if a killer does have a mental disorder, this does not, we repeat does *not,* equal insanity. Mental illness is a prerequisite for the insanity defense, but, like the sizes at Zara, it simply is not enough.

As clinical psychologist Laurence Miller puts it in his 2012 textbook *Criminal Psychology: Nature, Nurture, Culture:* "The mere presence, absence, or severity of any mental disorder does not by itself make a legal determination of insanity. Just because you're 'crazy' doesn't mean you didn't know what you were doing."

The specific rules around the insanity defense are *crazy (pun very much intended)* complicated and have evolved over time. So, to decipher these rules, we're going to compare and contrast two cases that from the outside look very similar: the cases of Andrea Yates and Susan Smith. Both involve a mother killing her children; both women drowned their children; both women suffered from mental illness and had previously tried to kill themselves. And, both defense teams attempted to use a not guilty by reason of insanity defense. Yet the legal outcomes were worlds apart.

To compare these cases, let's first consider the murders each woman committed, then the women's backgrounds leading up to the crimes, and finally, we'll analyze both of their insanity defenses.

The Murders

ANDREA YATES

On June 20, 2001, Rusty Yates was at work when he received a call from his wife, Andrea. "Come home, it's about the kids."

Rusty was confused. "Is there something wrong with them? Which ones?"

To which Andrea replied, "All of them."

Rusty rushed home, but when he arrived, he froze in fear at the sight of police cars surrounding his house. Before Andrea had phoned Rusty that day, she had called the Houston PD to tell them that she had killed all five of her children.

When the police arrived, the 37-year-old former nurse was calm; she let them in and told them again that she had killed her children. With that, Andrea Yates sat down on the couch in the front hallway with a disconnected, faraway gaze in her eyes and stopped speaking altogether. The house was dead silent. The officers at the scene started walking from room to room. They had no idea what they'd find; here was a woman who had confessed to something unbelievable, and then had become completely unresponsive. This was like no situation they had ever encountered.

The first responders made their way through the house, and finally one officer entered the master bedroom. On the bed he saw what he thought was a doll peeking out from under the sheet, but when he pulled down the covers, he was aghast. Four little bodies lay side by side. The officer who made the discovery was in a state of shock, but he noticed that the children's bodies were soaking wet, and instinctively he walked into the bathroom. Here he found another child's body floating face down in the bathtub. Andrea had drowned all five of her young children.

Rusty didn't yet know this, but he did know that something was very wrong because the police wouldn't let him in. He was outside his house banging his fists and screaming at Andrea, "What have you done?" over and over again. All the while, on the other side of the door, Andrea just sat there staring with the same blank look on her face. The police were at a total loss; it's not often that women kill their own children and it's even less common that when they do, they just sit there silently waiting to be arrested.

The police took Andrea into custody. Once at the station, she gave an 18-minute-long confession during which she spoke mainly about the devil and hell, saying of her children, "Maybe in their innocent years God would take them up to be in heaven." Throughout her confession, Andrea remained entirely calm.

When asked during her psychological evaluation, "If you hadn't taken their lives what would have happened?" Andrea told doctors, "They would have continued stumbling and ended up in hell."

As you can see, the case of Andrea Yates is a bizarre and heartbreaking one, and it only gets sadder and stranger as we take a look at Andrea's history and the years leading up to that dark day. But before we go there, we're going to leave Andrea for the moment and hop over to the small town of Union, South Carolina and to Susan Smith.

SUSAN SMITH

At around 3:30 p.m. on October 25, 1994, 23-year-old Susan Smith left Conso Products, where she worked as a secretary. She went to pick up her two sons, three-year-old Michael and 14-month-old Alexander. She returned home with the boys at 6 p.m. She fed the kids dinner and then sometime between 7:30 p.m. and 8 p.m. she strapped both children into her black Mazda Protege and went for a drive. Soon Susan was banging on the door of a house near the John D. Long Lake. *(A lake named after Ku Klux Klan member and State Senator John D. Long . . . cool.)* Susan was hysterical; the family at the house called 911.

When the police arrived, Susan told them that she had just been out for a drive to visit a friend and then to go to Walmart. On the way, she was stopped at a traffic light when, according to Susan, a Black man threatened her with a gun. She claimed that he broke into the car, jammed the gun into her ribs, and told her to drive or he'd kill her. Sobbing uncontrollably, Susan explained that the mystery man had made her drive out of town for about 10 minutes, all the while with the gun in her side and with her kids screaming in the back. Eventually they reached the access road to the lake where the man told Susan to get out of the car. She said she pleaded with the man to let her get her sons, but he drove off with the kids still crying in the back of the car.

The report of a Black man kidnapping two white children in South Carolina meant a massive search for the carjacker kicked off immediately. Roadblocks went up and cars everywhere were being stopped and checked. Susan was inconsolable and the residents of Union were heartbroken for her and her family. Over the following nine days, the police searched everywhere but found nothing. There was no trace of the mystery assailant, Susan's car, or her kids.

Susan spent her time making tearful appearances on television begging for the return of her children. She even worked with a police sketch artist—a composite drawing of the suspect was broadcast nationwide. But soon the police started to have their doubts about Susan. In the book *Sins of the Mother*, Maria Eftimiades explains how suspicions began to arise when police realized that Susan's description of her attacker was super generic and also the friend she said she was going to visit hadn't even been at home that day. And although most of the time Susan seemed hysterical, when investigators looked at her closely they weren't sure they could see any real tears.

Susan also failed a polygraph test, which raised some major police eyebrows. *But* if you've ever listened to our podcast, you'll know that we don't put much stock in lie detectors or polygraphs because they just don't work. (Want to know why? See the sidebar below.)

THE BIG LIE DETECTOR LIE

Lie detectors, also known as polygraphs, don't work because there is *no* universal physical or physiological response to deception, so how could a machine possibly *measure* it? Psychology professor Aldert Vrij at the University of Portsmouth, who is an expert on this topic, told the BBC in 2018, "It [the lie detector] does not measure deception, which is the core problem." Polygraphs look out for increased sweating, an elevated heart rate, and erratic breathing, but none of these responses are indicative only of lying; there could be so many other reasons for them.

Rather than being signs of deception, these responses are usually just signs of stress. So giving someone who has just been through a stressful or traumatic experience a polygraph is pointless. Finally, some people *aren't* stressed by lying, even if they have done something horrific and are being questioned by the police. Someone with psychopathic tendencies, for example, is very unlikely to have a stress-related physical response when lying or deceiving *(or waving back at someone who wasn't waving at them).* So lie detectors should probably just get in the bin.

Although the lie detector results that made the police doubt Susan's story were pretty pointless, the police were in fact right to be suspicious. Whenever investigators would question Susan and hint at the possibility that she might have been involved in her children's disappearance, she would totally fucking lose it and become incredibly belligerent. They didn't believe her version of events anymore, but without anything else to go on, they had to continue the search for the missing children.

On the ninth day of the search, after giving yet another emotional appeal on television, Susan Smith finally broke down in a police interrogation. She fell to the floor crying and confessed that her kids were at the bottom of John D. Long Lake. Within hours police divers found her black Mazda 18 feet underwater, 122 feet from shore. Alex and Michael were still inside.

Susan Smith claimed that she had been feeling suicidal and had gone out to the lake to kill herself and the boys, but only because she didn't want them to live without a mother. According to Susan, that night had been a culmination of weeks of depression. She put the kids in the car and drove around for hours before finally stopping at the lake, where she decided to end it all. However, Susan said then "something happened": she got out of the car, took the hand brake off, and let the car roll down the ramp and into the lake, taking her little boys with it.

As you can see, there are some similarities to Susan Smith and Andrea Yates's stories, such as the fact that both women seemed to know that what they had done was legally wrong, seeing as how Andrea Yates called the police to confess and Susan Smith tried a cover-up. But there are also many differences between the women, such as in their behaviors in the immediate aftermath of the killings.

Let's consider their backgrounds. What had happened in the years leading up to the point that Andrea Yates and Susan Smith each did what they did? And are they actually "insane," or just "crazy"?

Backgrounds

ANDREA YATES

Andrea had been brought up in Houston and was a fantastic overachiever. She excelled in academics, sports, everything. She was captain of the swim team, a historian of the National Honor Society, and even class valedictorian her senior year.

After high school, Andrea went to the University of Texas to study nursing and went on to land her dream job. In 1989, at age 25, Andrea met her future husband Rusty Yates. Rusty was also 25, had a bloody cool name, and had a great job working as a computer systems designer for NASA. As far as Andrea was concerned, he was a catch. After three years of dating the pair got married. From the outside they seemed like the perfect couple, but behind closed doors, things weren't going great. As Suzy Spencer explains in her book on the case, *Breaking Point*, according to Rusty, Andrea hated sex. He had hoped that things would get better after they got married, but they didn't.

For a couple seemingly struggling with intimacy, they got pregnant pretty fast, and on February 26, 1994, their first child, Noah, was born. Almost immediately after Noah's birth, Andrea began to experience some weird symptoms. She started having violent thoughts and hearing voices that she believed to be the devil. Andrea was terrified, so she didn't tell anyone what was going on. Meanwhile, Rusty, not noticing that there was an issue, wanted to try for another baby. He jokingly called Andrea "Fertile Myrtle." The very next year Andrea got pregnant again, and on December 15, 1995, the couple had another son, John.

With a second baby now in the picture, Andrea's stress levels went through the roof and so did her violent fantasies. But again, Andrea suppressed it all—and things were about to get a whole lot worse. In 1996, Rusty got a job in Florida. He then made a terrible decision that further eroded Andrea's mental health. (Again, Andrea hadn't told anyone yet what was happening to her, but Rusty hadn't noticed, either.) Rusty moved his fragile wife—who by this point was regularly hearing voices and having visions of violence—and his two young sons into a 38-foot trailer.

Now there's nothing wrong with living in a trailer, and as we'll see this isn't the main reason why Andrea spiraled, but it certainly didn't help. The move into the trailer wasn't an economic decision; Rusty worked for NASA and had the money to move them into a house. But the thing is, Andrea wasn't the only one worried about the devil. Back in college, Rusty had started following the teachings of Michael Woroniecki—a very fire-and-brimstone street preacher—who even dabbled in a bit of Christ-centric EDM on the side. Woroniecki describes himself as an independent, nondenominational Christian missionary, and back in the nineties he and his wife Rachel left Michigan with their six kids and hit the road in a bus-shaped church on wheels for some Jesus-themed *Wild Thornberrys* fun!

They traveled all over the US (and a bunch of other countries, too) preaching on street corners, spreading their particular brand of Christianity—one of austerity, biblical back to basics, and the idea that only a very few, very select group of people can ascend to heaven. *(In a bit of a bummer, everyone else goes to hell.)* This austerity teaching was key to their whole deal; and it was perhaps this idea that convinced the Yates family to leave their nice house in the suburbs and move into that trailer.

The year they made the trailer their home, Andrea got pregnant again and miscarried. But it wasn't long before she was pregnant once more. In 1997 the Yateses had their third son, Paul. After this, Andrea's visions got worse and the voices intensified: they started telling Andrea to kill her children. But still, Rusty didn't notice anything wrong with his wife.

The following year, with the boys getting bigger by the day, Rusty traded in the trailer for an old 350-square-foot Greyhound bus. And if three boys and two adults living on a bus wasn't enough, just a few months later baby number four, Luke, arrived. The conditions on the bus were dire, but Rusty was at work all the time and it was Andrea who was left at home on the bus every day, alone with four boys under the age of four. She wouldn't even use disposable diapers or a washing machine, again to maintain a simple and austere life. Andrea felt like she was drowning. The voices were now screaming at her.

The 2002 *Mugshots* episode "A Mother's Madness" makes clear how Andrea's life was unraveling; she was homeschooling her three eldest boys and nursing a newborn, all while living on a bus. Andrea was also now pen-paling the Woronieckis—although it had been Rusty who had brought the preacher into their lives, Andrea Yates was now the one following his teachings with the zeal of a convert.

Slowly but surely over that summer, Andrea's delusions began to deepen and merge with the biblical mumbo jumbo she was regularly consuming. And boy was there a lot of mumbo jumbo. According to Dr. Lucy Puryear, an expert witness hired by Yates's defense team, Woroniecki's key message to his followers was, "If you think you're a good person and a Christian and that you're going to heaven, you aren't, because that's prideful and only God knows and chooses who goes to heaven." He also believed that all women are evil; he even wrote to Andrea telling her that she was the daughter of Eve and a wicked witch. This guy had absolutely zero fucking chill, and as you can imagine, these sorts of messages just made things worse.

By now, people had started to notice that something was wrong with Andrea, but still she didn't get the help that she needed. Andrea was becoming more and more isolated, and she was still regularly communicating with Woroniecki.

It was the perfect storm: Michael Woroniecki was delivering messages of good, evil, God, and the devil, and to Andrea's fracturing mind it all made perfect sense. As mentioned above, from Dr. Puryear's statements in court, Woroniecki had a specific problem with how modern women raised their children and it was this particular belief that Andrea latched on to. According to Woroniecki, it's the woman's job to stay at home and raise the kids, but women today are just too lazy to bring up their kids right. He even wrote a whimsical little poem about it, which he published in his terribly named newsletter *The Perilous Times*. This poem, which ends with the harrowing lines, "Modern mother worldly cast in hell! Now what becomes of the children of such a Jezebel?" had been sent to Andrea in the days leading up to the murders and it was used as evidence at trial by both the prosecution and the defense.

Thanks to this kind of rhetoric, Andrea started to see herself as the "Jezebel" and her kids as the ones who would pay the price for her failures. She became convinced that her kids would go to hell because she was a terrible mother, even though everyone who knew her thought she was a loving, warm, and natural mom. But this is how psychosis works; things that a psychotic person may have been exposed to—like religion—become key manifestations of their delusions. In Andrea's case, as her psychosis was taking hold, she was simultaneously being bombarded with extreme messages—of good, evil, God, and the devil—and so the two became enmeshed.

Four months after Luke was born, Rusty got a call from Andrea who said simply, "Come home, I need help." When Rusty got home (to the bus), Andrea was sitting there chewing her fingers—not her fingernails, her fingers—and she was shaking. By this point Andrea had been having vivid, intrusive thoughts about killing the kids for months. It was consuming her.

Rusty took Andrea and the kids to Andrea's parents' house—he was at a loss about what to do. And while being off that bus was a good start, Andrea still needed medical help. The next day, Andrea intentionally overdosed on her father's sleeping pills. She was in freefall, but she survived.

Following the suicide attempt, Andrea was taken to a psychiatric hospital, diagnosed with major depressive disorder, and prescribed the antidepressant Zoloft. Andrea was then referred to psychiatrist Dr. Eileen Starbranch, who recommended changing Andrea's medication to the antipsychotic Zyprexa. Andrea needed all the help she could get, but she was still trapped in the Woroniecki bubble—and according to him, all doctors were bad and medication was even worse. So Andrea, who was in a deeply paranoid state of psychosis, secretly stopped taking her medication. She began regressing: She started pulling out her own hair, scratching at her skin relentlessly, and tearing at the sores and scabs on her body. Andrea's visual and auditory hallucinations also began to intensify. She would hear the words "get a knife, get a knife, get a knife" screaming over and over in her head.

After weeks of this, one day Andrea did get a knife. But, terrified that she was going to kill her children, she tried to stab *herself* in the neck. This time, Rusty saw her, and he managed to wrestle the knife away and take Andrea back to the hospital. She admitted to doctors that she had had the knife hallucination more than 10 times in the previous few days. Finally, Andrea was diagnosed with postpartum psychosis and given an emergency dose of the powerful antipsychotic drug Haldol. (What is postpartum psychosis? We explain in the sidebar below.)

WHAT IS POSTPARTUM PSYCHOSIS?

Postpartum psychosis is not the same as postpartum depression. Postpartum depression *is* a serious disorder, but it is quite common; up to one in seven women can experience the feelings of persistent sadness, anxiety, and a lack of energy that comes with postpartum depression. But according to the NHS (the UK's National Health Service), postpartum *psychosis* only occurs in one out of every one thousand births. In these cases, women will suffer from delusions, hallucinations, and a manic mood; essentially the symptoms we'd see in someone who is psychotic. Over half of women diagnosed with postpartum psychosis go on to be diagnosed with bipolar disorder or manic depression, but most women with postpartum psychosis do make a full recovery as long as they receive the right treatment. The right treatment being medication, therapy, and in some very severe cases, electroconvulsive therapy (ECT), which involves small electric currents being passed through the brain to induce seizures and alter brain chemistry.

Andrea's psychiatrist recommended that she have ECT, but she and Rusty decided against it, so after three weeks in the hospital Andrea was released with prescriptions for the necessary medications and with a plan for her to have monthly check-ins with her doctor. She and Rusty were also told in no uncertain terms to not have any more children, something Dr. Starbranch, Andrea's psychiatrist, has confirmed and reiterated in every interview she has given over the years. This is because when a woman has already had an episode of postpartum psychosis, she has a 50 to 80 percent chance of having *another* episode if she has another baby. And not only does the risk of a psychotic episode increase, but the symptoms are likely to be even worse and much harder to treat.

Back on her medication and now living with her family in a nice new house, Andrea started to improve. By September 1999, her condition had improved considerably and she was getting back to her old self. Two months later, Andrea and Rusty made a fateful decision. Against her doctor's advice Andrea stopped taking her birth control and her antipsychotic medication. The following year, the couple's fifth child and first daughter, Mary, was born.

On May 31, 2001, Andrea was taken back to the hospital, diagnosed with major depressive disorder, and—no surprise—postpartum psychosis. This time, however, Andrea didn't improve. But not knowing what to do,

Rusty took Andrea home with yet more prescriptions for antipsychotics and antidepressants. Within months, all five of the Yates children would be dead and Andrea would be in jail.

SUSAN SMITH

Now that we understand a little more about Andrea's background, what about Susan Smith's? What led up to the point that she killed her two sons?

Susan was born on September 26, 1971 in Union, South Carolina. Right from the start, her life was anything but stable. When she was seven her mother and father separated, and just a few weeks later, her mom married another man named Beverly Russell.

Shortly thereafter, Susan's father took his own life; and Susan—who had always been a bubbly child—became sullen, withdrawn, and quiet. She struggled with depression and even made a suicide attempt at age 13. But as a teenager Susan became good at hiding her pain. She was a popular and outgoing student, even voted "Friendliest Female" *(whatever the hell that means)* in her senior year of high school.

At the time, from the outside it looked like Susan had it all—a loving middle-class family; doing well at school; she seemed happy. But Susan wasn't happy. When she had turned 16, allegations were made that her stepfather Beverly Russell had started sexually abusing her. Susan actually reported the abuse to Child Protective Services and Russell was removed from the house. But after just a few family counseling sessions he was allowed to return home, because Susan refused to press charges. The question that needs to be screamed in the faces of the people who made this decision is why on earth, even if a teenage girl doesn't want to press charges, would no action be taken against a man who is suspected of abusing her? In fact, Susan's mother stayed with Russell. So nothing changed, life returned to "normal," and Russell continued to sexually abuse his stepdaughter.

As a teenager, Susan worked at a supermarket; her outwardly upbeat personality made her a hit with the customers. During this time she had affairs with a much older married man and with another co-worker. At 18, Susan got pregnant and had an abortion, but this scared the married man and he called off their relationship. Susan couldn't cope and she tried to kill herself again by overdosing on painkillers. Susan was not OK, but no one in her life seems to have cared.

In March 1991, when Susan discovered that she was pregnant again, she decided to marry the baby's father, her co-worker and high school friend David Smith. David actually wrote a book in 1995, *Beyond All Reason,* in which he details how the next few years of his and Susan's life unfolded. According to him their relationship was a volatile and unstable one.

On October 10, 1991, their first son, Michael, was born. But things were not smooth sailing; by the following March, David and Susan had separated. Still, they kept sleeping together, and by the end of the year Susan was pregnant once again. At this point she and David decided to get back together, and Susan insisted that buying their own place would solve a lot of their problems. They borrowed money from Susan's mom and bought a house, but in what would become an ongoing problem in their marriage, Susan always wanted a lot more (materialistically speaking) than her or David's income could provide. This put a huge amount of pressure on their relationship, so despite the new house and a second baby on the way, Susan and David started to drift apart.

Over the course of the next few months, they split up and got back together again twice. It was during this turbulent time that their son Alexander was born, on August 5, 1993. Unfortunately, within a few weeks, the

Smiths decided to call it quits on their marriage for good. During their entire relationship Susan and David had carried on working together at the supermarket where they had first met. *You have to wonder, with all the arguments these two had how the hell they managed it, but they did.* But perhaps Susan had finally had enough because it was at this point that she took a new job at Conso Products, where she rapidly climbed the ranks to personal assistant to the CEO.

Finally, many of Susan's desires started to come true: she was now rubbing shoulders with the elites of South Carolina. She saw how the other half lived and she liked it. Susan was thrilled when she started a casual relationship with her boss' son, Tom Findlay. But with this cast of characters, things are about as simple as the plot of *Lost (and spoiler: the ending is just as shit)* and by spring 1994, Susan was once again also seeing David.

We'd imagine it was a nightmare keeping up this new weird love triangle, and after a few months of giving it a go, Susan suddenly asked David for a divorce and tried to step things up with Tom. However, if Susan thought that this would keep Tom by her side, she was mistaken. As Susan was finalizing her divorce, he was backing out, and on October 17, 1994, Tom Findlay wrote Susan a letter ending their relationship. He told her that they were just too different—he didn't want to have children, and he certainly didn't want to raise *hers*. The letter finished with a bit of advice that is just the most cringe shit you'll ever read: "If you want to catch a nice guy like me one day you have to act like a nice girl. And you know, nice girls don't sleep with married men." *(Here, Tom is referring to Susan's sexual relationships with other men in town, but he doesn't seem too hard on himself for sleeping with a very married Susan . . . funny that. But don't worry, we have already forwarded this to @beam_me_up_softboi.)*

After Tom ended their relationship, Susan became depressed again and went back to sleeping with David, her abusive stepfather Beverly Russell, and even Tom's dad (her boss). October 1994 was a rough month for Susan Smith and it was the beginning of the end. She was desperate to get Tom back so she tried everything she could think of. She told him that Russell had been sexually abusing her since she was a teenager, and when Tom didn't seem to care, she told him that she was going to tell everyone about her affair with his father. Unsurprisingly, this threat also failed to win Tom's love, and he told Susan it was never going to happen.

It was later revealed to police, and exposed at trial, that during this time Susan had casually mentioned to a friend, "I wonder what my life would be like if I didn't have kids . . ." If this had been a thought on Susan's mind, she wouldn't have to wait long to find out. On October 25, just 10 days after Tom Findlay had ended their relationship, Susan drove her two sons into John D. Long Lake.

After having lied for over a week that a Black man had hijacked her car, Susan had finally confessed everything. When divers found her car at the bottom of the lake with Michael and Alex's bodies in the backseat, the breakup letter from Tom Findlay was discovered in the glove compartment.

Much to everyone's surprise, at first David Smith stood by Susan. He told everyone she must have been out of her mind. He knew about her difficult childhood, the sexual abuse, the depression, and the multiple attempts she had made on her own life. But any sympathy David had for his former wife would soon vanish.

Insane, or Just Crazy?

Before we get to the trials of Andrea Yates and Susan Smith, let's talk about insanity. As we said at the start of this chapter, insanity is a legal term, not a clinical one. Not guilty by reason of insanity (NGRI) is a defense used by a person who is claiming that they are not *criminally* responsible for their crimes. To understand what that actually means in the eyes of the law, we're going to have to throw some real legal definition grenades at you, so pull on your smart pants and pay attention.

The law uses the term *insane* to refer to a very specific set of conditions under which *some* seriously mentally ill people are deemed not responsible for having committed criminal acts. We have to say again *(and guys, we're going to keep banging on about this)* these conditions only apply to *some* mentally ill people. Mental illness and insanity are not synonymous. To be found NGRI, you *must* have a mental illness, but that alone is not sufficient. Therefore, not all seriously mentally ill people who commit crimes are legally insane at the time they did whatever they did.

Why? It's all about intent. In a court of law, you have to show that the accused had *intent*, or the ability to form intent, for there to be a crime. Without evidence of intent, even if the outcome is the same (someone was killed, for example), the case can't be tried in the same way as if there had been intent.

Essentially NGRI means that the person either did not know what they were doing, or did not know that what they were doing was wrong. The problem is, as we'll see when we analyze the cases in this chapter, *wrong* is a very subjective word. Wrong by whose standards? Wrong is a very philosophical idea; what if someone's mental illness skews their perception of reality to the point that they have a definition of right and wrong that is no longer aligned with our societal sensibilities? Tricky, right? Don't worry, it gets worse.

Generally speaking, if the defense wants to go with an NGRI plea at trial, there are two requirements:

❶ They need expert testimony to show that the defendant is mentally ill.

❷ They need to be able to prove how this mental illness removed the defendant's ability to reason, their ability to understand what they were doing, or their ability to have intent.

For a defendant to be declared insane, their mental illness needs to have skewed their perception of reality to the extent that (1) they did not know what they were doing was illegal; (2) they didn't know what they were doing at all; *or* (3) they were being compelled to act by an irresistible force (like voices or visual hallucinations). Proof of one of these factors is absolutely central to this defense. Precisely which of these conditions needs to be proven will depend on the state—and don't worry, we're getting to that!

If someone is mentally ill but that mental illness did *not* remove their ability to understand what they were doing, and if they still had intent to commit the crime, they *cannot* be found not guilty by reason of insanity. Because, say it with us: *mental illness alone is not sufficient for an NGRI defense.* So, having a mental disorder doesn't make you a killer or violent, and having a mental disorder also doesn't automatically make you "insane" and therefore not responsible for your actions. Got it? Good.

Now let's talk about the rules and specific conditions one has to meet in order to be found insane in a court of law. These conditions are not uniform; they differ from country to country, and within the US, from state to state. This zip code lottery is important to remember, because it means that someone found insane in one state may not have been able to successfully claim NGRI had their case been tried elsewhere.

About half of the states in the US, and the UK and Canada, use what's known as the M'Naghten Rule. The other half of US states use the Model Penal Code. (Except New Hampshire, which decided to do its own thing and follows the Durham Rule. Live Free or Die indeed.)

MINI HISTORY SIDEBAR!

The M'Naghten Rule is the oldest of these conditions for NGRI. It dates all the way back to 1843 in jolly old England, when a Scottish wood turner named Daniel M'Naghten tried to assassinate the then prime minister of the UK, Robert Peel. But he ended up shooting and killing Peel's secretary, Edward Drummond, instead. At trial M'Naghten was found to be totally delusional, as he was convinced that he was being spied on and that the government was conspiring against him. It was a watershed moment in British legal history when he was found not guilty on the grounds of insanity.

Daniel M'Naghten was sent to a mental institution for the rest of his life, but people were pissed. They felt like he got away with it. Even Queen Victoria tried to get involved and have the decision changed, but it was a no-go.

So what is the definition of the M'Naghten Rule? It is probably what most of us think of when we think of the insanity defense—it is the argument that the defendant did not know what they were doing at the time of committing the offense, or if they did know, they were unable to discern right from wrong because of a defect of reason brought on by a disease of the mind.

Today, states that use the M'Naghten Rule can choose to do so with or without the addition of another rule, the Irresistible Impulse Test, which was introduced in the 1960s in the US. This test was created to help courts in situations where a defendant understood that what they were doing was wrong at the time they committed the crime, but due to a mental disease, they were unable to control themselves from doing said wrong thing.

Neither of these rules are perfect, not by a long shot. And they get super messy, so let's clarify the issues with each of them before we move on:

❶ The M'Naghten Rule is based upon the idea of "wrongfulness," but there is disagreement on whether this difference between right and wrong is a legal one or a moral one. *(Put a pin in this because it becomes very important later.)*

❷ The Irresistible Impulse Test's main issue is that there is little sci-entific evidence to back up the claim that mental illnesses (even when severe and genuine) can inhibit self-control to the point that the person had no other choice.

The other half of US states that allow the insanity defense use the Model Penal Code, which is actually much broader, and therefore a little more lenient than the M'Naghten Rule, because it allows for the nuances of morality and what is "wrong" to be taken into account.

So, how does all this apply to Andrea Yates and Susan Smith? Let's find out.

The Trials

ANDREA YATES

Andrea Yates was tried in Texas; Texas uses the M'Naghten Rule with the Irresistible Impulse Test, and the burden of proof of insanity is on the defendant.

Yates's stance from the start was that she needed to be punished. She wanted to plead guilty because she believed that she was a terrible mother. She also thought that when the state punished her for the murders, Satan himself would be destroyed. Of course, on hearing her plan, Yates's defense attorney Wendell Odom convinced her to plead not guilty by reason of insanity instead.

During her police interviews, Yates told officers that she loved her kids, but that she kept hearing voices that told her she was the devil. And because of her evil all of her children were destined for hell and eternal damnation. Yates felt that this was all predetermined—there was nothing she would be able to do to correct the path of sin her children were certain to follow. In her mind, the only way she could save the souls of her children was by sending them to heaven while they were still pure.

The defense's psychiatrist diagnosed Yates with cacodemonomania, the belief that one is possessed by evil spirits. But Yates told him that she wasn't just possessed by any old garden-variety demon—she was possessed by the "one and only Satan."

On February 18, 2002, Andrea Yates was finally deemed fit to stand trial; her defense team had prepared for an insanity defense while the State prosecution was getting ready to go after Yates hard—they were seeking the death penalty. The State decided that the best way to win their case was to try and keep the jury focused completely on whether Yates knew right from wrong as she killed her five children, one by one. They did not want the jury to be "distracted" by Yates's long history of mental illness. The State claimed that Yates *knew* what she was doing, because she was prepared, and they focused on the physical evidence.

One of their major points was that they could prove that Noah, the eldest child, was killed last. They claimed that this was because Yates knew he would put up the biggest fight and that might have alerted the other kids to what was about to happen. The prosecution was trying to show that Yates was aware of what she was doing and making reasoned decisions. *(But you could also argue that if you were going to commit mass murder because God needed you to, you'd take out the biggest threat first.)*

The defense had also an issue of optics to contend with; when Yates had first been arrested, Odom, her defense attorney, said that she was the "sickest woman he'd ever seen," but after months of medication and care she was looking much better. Of course, the jury was *meant* to be focusing on the defendant's state of mind at the time the offense was actually committed—but with Yates now looking almost "normal," how this came across at trial was definitely a factor to consider. And so, the defense showed the jury all the videos of Yates seeming totally unhinged just after her arrest. She was shown talking about cartoon characters speaking to her through the TV, telling her to kill her children to save them from hell.

Obviously both sides had their own expert psychiatric witnesses; the defense had Dr. Phillip Resnick and the prosecution had Dr. Park Dietz. (Dr. Dietz is arguably one of the most high-profile forensic psychiatrists in the world; he's worked on cases like that of Joel Rifkin, Jeffrey Dahmer, and the Unabomber, and he even works as an advisor for TV shows like *Law & Order.*)

During their assessments, both Dr. Resnick and Dr. Dietz agreed that Yates was indeed sick. Check one! We have the first necessary condition met. Both doctors also agreed that Yates knew what she did was against the law. After all, Yates had called 911 straight away, turned herself in, and immediately confessed. But Dr. Resnick argued that although Yates knew what she had done was legally wrong, she thought it was *morally* right. Although she had a conceptualization of right and wrong, Yates was so plagued by religious delusions, her beliefs so manifest, that essentially the two had been flipped.

Dr. Dietz disagreed. He told the court that Yates knew what she did was wrong in the eyes of the law—and crucially, in the eyes of God. Dr. Dietz also gave the court his opinion on how Yates had come up with her plan to commit murder. He claimed that the same week she had killed her children, an episode of *Law & Order* had aired that featured the storyline of a woman who drowned her child to escape her responsibilities. He said that Yates must have seen this show and been inspired, and he knew it was a great and inspiring storyline because he had of course consulted on that particular episode.

After three weeks of testimony and videos of Yates talking about demons, the jury deliberated for just three and a half hours and returned with a verdict of guilty—but at sentencing they decided to spare her life.

Under the rigid M'Naghten Rule that Texas applies, there is no room for discussions about the difference between *morally* wrong and *legally* wrong. But had Yates been tried in a state that used the Model Penal Code, it's very likely that she would have been found not guilty by reason of insanity. Under this rule, her defense team could have *successfully* made the case that although Yates knew what she had done was *criminal*, and that society would condemn her acts as wrong, that society wouldn't think she was actually a criminal if only they understood what she was "aware" of (i.e., that God had told her that she *had* to kill her kids to save them from burning in hellfire for all eternity).

We must not forget the victims: Noah, John, Luke, Mary, and Paul—the five Yates children. But we do believe that Yates is also a victim. She had needed help for years, and tragically, her mental condition directly interfered with her seeking the necessary medical care. We believe that Andrea Yates should have been found not guilty by reason of insanity. If you agree, hold on to your hats. Because the story isn't over yet . . .

After the trial, questions quickly arose about Dr. Dietz's testimony—not about his assessment of Yates's mental illness, but about the episode of *Law & Order* he had cited. Yates's defense team pored over every single script of the show, and they couldn't find any episode like the one Dietz had described. The defense also found 19 points of error from the first trial, and finally on June 26, 2006, Andrea Yates got her retrial. After a month of testimony, the jury spent 13 hours deliberating before delivering their verdict.

Five years after the murders, Andrea Yates was finally found not guilty by reason of insanity. In the years between Yates's original conviction and her retrial there had been a huge shift in people's understanding of postpartum psychosis, and this definitely played a large part in her getting a new verdict—what we believe was the right verdict—the second time around.

Yates was sent to Kerrville State Hospital for treatment; she is still there today and there is no timetable for her release. The only way for her to ever be released would be to pass a psychiatric review that would assess if she was likely to be a danger to herself or anyone else, but Yates has refused every opportunity to do so because she still believes that she should be punished.

Now, stop splashing your tears on this book, get a tissue, wipe your face, and let's get on to Susan Smith's trial.

SUSAN SMITH

Just as with Andrea Yates, across the country there was a palpable sense of rage toward Susan Smith in the wake of her children's drownings, so the prosecution in South Carolina went after the death penalty.

The trial kicked off on July 17, 1995, and Smith pleaded NGRI. It should have been a relatively easy case for the prosecution; after all, like Texas, South Carolina also uses the M'Naghten Rule and the burden of proof for insanity is on the defendant. Smith had also confessed in writing to murdering Alex and Michael.

But the prosecution majorly fucked up when they decided to try and show *why* Smith had killed her kids. There was no need for them to show a motive; they just had to prove that she *had done it.* Perhaps this decision was down to the prosecution wanting to undermine Smith's insanity defense by pointing out a sordid and very practical motive. Whatever the reason, they ran with the theory that Smith had killed her sons so that she could get back together with Tom Findlay. After all, Findlay had dumped her because of her kids—the letter found in the car proved that.

This attempt to show motive allowed the defense an opportunity to make a much stronger argument than they could have otherwise. David Bruck, Smith's defense attorney, wanted to show the jury that Smith wasn't evil. She didn't kill her kids to be with Tom Findlay; she was a loving mom. She was just sick, depressed, and suicidal.

He claimed that Smith had been in the car and drove it halfway down the ramp into the lake before stopping and getting out. Then something terrible happened and the car rolled into the lake and killed the boys. Smith had been out of her mind at the time of the killings; she wasn't thinking straight. Bruck then told the jury about how Smith's father had killed himself when she was six years old and how her stepfather had started to sexually abuse her from the age of 15, with the last incident occurring just three months before the boys had drowned. Smith was battling alcoholism as a result of her extensive traumas and Findlay's breaking things off had pushed her into another severe bout of depression.

This narrative moved the case away from being an open-and-shut, cold-blooded, premeditated cash-grab. Susan Smith was now a sympathetic character, and the case was more complicated than completing the *New York Times* crossword with a hangover. But, as we said, South Carolina uses the M'Naghten Rule, and the prosecution could easily show that Smith had known what she had done was wrong. Right from the start, within minutes of the killings, Smith was lying to everyone, including to the police.

The prosecution showed the jury an experiment on how long it would take a car like Smith's to fully submerge—she had had six minutes to save her kids and didn't. Smith was able to show investigators exactly where the car was, meaning she must have stood and watched it sink. So it's hard to argue that it was an accident or that she didn't know what she was doing, especially as she waited until the car was fully submerged before she went running to a nearby house, crying hysterical tears, to recount her carjacking story.

So, the trial came down to the following:

❶ Did Susan Smith have a mental disorder? I think we can safely say *yes*.

❷ Was she suffering from a mental disorder at the time of the crime? Possibly. Even likely, given her history.

❸ Did her mental illness interfere with her ability to know that what she was doing was wrong? We don't think so. Susan Smith lied to the police for nine days; she made up a completely false story about being abducted; and she led the police on a wild goose chase after a phantom Black man.

The jury felt much the same. On July 27, 1995, Susan Smith was sentenced to life in prison for the murders of her sons, Michael and Alexander, with the possibility of parole after 30 years. Smith claims to have remorse and says she didn't lie to protect herself; she lied to protect her ex-husband's parents. And she still says that she did not kill the kids because of Tom Findlay. She is adamant she was intending to kill herself, but she never explains why her sons ended up dead and not her. Smith tried to appeal her sentence in 2010 but failed.

If there's anything we have learned during our years doing our podcast, it's that the crossroads representing the intersection of law and mental health is a dangerous place to be standing. It's a bloody mess, and if you hang around there too long, something big, heavy, and existential-crisis-shaped is going to smash into you. Our aim with this chapter is to make clear there are many nuances to mental illness, and that there is a huge difference between diagnoses made to treat sick people and diagnoses made for a court of law.

And finally, we wanted to address a criticism often levied at the NGRI defense—that it's used as a tactic or a get out of jail free card. As you've seen, not only is it a very difficult defense to pull off, it also doesn't really benefit anyone except the truly "insane." Susan Smith has the chance for parole in 2024, but it's unlikely she'll get it as she hasn't exactly been the model prisoner. Andrea Yates has been committed to a mental hospital for an indeterminate amount of time, and while it's the best place for her as she is actually receiving the treatment she needs, she'll be there long-term. Susan Smith might get out, but Andrea Yates probably never will.

Remember, not guilty by reason of insanity doesn't mean freedom. And as the saying in legal circles goes: "You'd have to be insane to plead insanity."

4

MISOGYNY

Black Pills, Blue Balls, and Basement Virgins

EVERY FIBER OF OUR BEING WANTS TO SIMPLY LAUGH AT "incels" (involuntary celibates) and their deranged hatred of women. We want to roll our eyes and scoff at these basement-dwelling weirdos who sit around on their online forums, complaining that they are losing out in the "sexual marketplace" because of their weak chins and short legs, and who call women "femoids" (female humanoids). But increasingly, just mocking these men feels like a mistake.

Over the past few years, members of this strange and sad subculture have started to organize, and more concerningly, *radicalize*. Individuals who identify with the incel movement have committed horrific acts of real-life violence that can only be described as terrorism.

The latest figures from the FBI show that from 2015 to 2020, at least 50 murders in North America have been directly linked to incel-inspired violence. Incels are, without a doubt, one of the West's newest domestic terror threats, and as pathetic as these men are, as the body count linked to their ideology piles up, it's time we took them dead seriously.

In this chapter we are going to take a big old deep dive into the grimy waters of the "incelosphere," bask in the putrid glow of online misogynistic radicalization, and ask what drives the violence we've seen in recent years. While some people in the media want to just dismiss these men as jokes and losers (and don't get us wrong, they are most certainly *super* losers), there's so much more to this story. Journalist David Futrelle is an expert in all things manosphere (the toxic corner of the internet filled with anti-feminist propaganda that, according to a 2019 article in the *Atlantic*, has become "a recruiting ground for potential mass shooters"). We think Futrelle absolutely put it best when he said, "misogyny kills, quite literally."

Toronto Van Attack

While there are sadly many, many incidents of mass murder by incels that we could reference to kick off this chapter, let's start with April 23, 2018, in Toronto. This was the day a 25-year-old man named Alek Minassian drove a van into a crowd of people waiting outside a local tennis game. He killed 10 and injured 16 that day, and the fact that his victims were mostly women was no accident.

After the van attack Minassian was captured alive (despite his best attempts to end it all through suicide by cop), and he was arrested and taken in for questioning. It turned out that he was a former computer science student who had gone on to join—and then swiftly leave—the Canadian Armed Forces. If at first the police were confused by what had been behind this man's desire to carry out such a seemingly random attack, Minassian quickly made his motivations clear. He told investigators about his time on the incel forums of Reddit and 4chan, and explained through gritted teeth how angry he was at women—a rage he claimed had grown and festered after he had been rejected by a girl in 2012.

The year 2012 was six years before the attack! So Minassian was still furious about a rejection that had happened more than half a decade before, and he was using it to explain why he had just murdered 10 women. And it only got a whole lot more bizarre when Alek Minassian stated that he was a "supreme gentleman." He said he was angry that women would give their love and affection to all these "obnoxious brutes" instead of him. He then started telling the police that he knew a lot of other guys on the internet who felt the same way, but that they were just "too cowardly to act on their anger." He also said that he hoped his attack would motivate others to join him in what he called the "incel rebellion."

At the time of this attack, the world of incels was not very well known or understood. It was a strange and clandestine group, and a lot of the references and language that Minassian was using made little sense to outsiders. But soon, more clues began to emerge as to his motive. It turned out that just minutes before he had plowed his van into innocent people, Alek Minassian had uploaded the following post to Facebook:

> Private Recruit Minassian Infantry 00010, wishing to speak to Sgt 4chan please. C23249161. The Incel Rebellion has already begun! We will overthrow all the Chads and Stacys! All hail the supreme gentleman Elliot Rodger!

Who the hell is Elliot Rodger? Well, he's the founding father of modern online inceldom, the poster boy for the movement—the grand high wizard of being a dick who hates women. He earned himself these illustrious titles when he killed six people and injured 14 others in Isla Vista, California in 2014. And like all horrendously self-important wankers, Rodger left behind a screed—a 141-page manifesto called "My Twisted World," in which he raged about women and explained in great detail his desire to get revenge on the entire female population. This piece of literary genius really stuck, and today it has become something of a bible for the incel community.

But before we get to King Dweeb Elliot Rodger, the man himself, a forewarning: This chapter is going to need a lot of glossary-ing. You may have noticed that the message Minassian posted on Facebook doesn't make a whole lot of sense. Well, incels are a pretty insular bunch with a very specific set of ideologies and a very—shall we say—esoteric, meme-heavy way of communicating. So in order for us to really understand the crimes committed by members of this group, we have to come to grips with a lot of strange terminology. Prepare yourself to be smacked in the face with a ton of new and very weird lingo.

Dickhead Dictionary

Incels ("involuntary celibates") are (mostly) men who are unable to find a romantic and sexual partner—even though they want one and believe that they have tried to get one. Crucially, they feel that women are to blame for their lack of spousal success. And so, one key unifying trait of incels, at the very heart of incel philosophy, is a deep-seated grievance toward all women.

These men are angry and bitter and live in a black-and-white world of their own creation in which one's appearance trumps everything else. Incels see sex as a commodity to be traded among the attractive. Incels believe that they lose out on sex because women are shallow and simple. In this worldview, sex is a zero-sum game: all men are fighting it out for sex and relationships with women, and one man's success is another man's loneliness.

So perhaps you're wondering, where might one find an incel in the wild? Well, they are a part of the dark and infinitely creepy corner of the internet known as the manosphere: a cesspit of misogyny, mildly amusing memes, horribly punctuated websites, and increasingly terrifying calls for brutal acts of violence against women—including mass rape. It's worth pointing out, in an ironic twist, that the word *incel* was actually coined in the 1990s by a female student called "Alana." She innocently started *Alana's Involuntary Celibacy Project* as an online group for lonely people to connect and support each other. However, the community seemed to fracture in the mid-2000s and a new misogynistic offshoot called Love Shy was born.

Since then, the term has been hijacked by these angry and aggrieved men who rage at women for not giving them the sex that they feel entitled to, and now "Alana" no longer has anything to do with the incel community. Today, most incels are men, and while female incels, referred to on online forums as "femcels," *do* exist, they are usually dismissed by their lonely male peers who do not believe that women can really be incels.

Now that we know the modern incel origin story, let's have a gander at the evolution of this group. By 2015, they were hanging out pretty openly on mainstream forums like Reddit, 4chan, and 8chan, and quickly their numbers boomed. They sat around on these sites talking about how outrageous it was that women denied them sex. Some (who clearly revered Elliot Rodger) also started to share their fantasies about violence, calling on their fellow incels to take part in random shootings and advocating for mass rape.

Pretty soon the violent fantasies started to spill over into real life, and incels were pushed out of places like Reddit. They were driven to start their own "safe space" forums like incels.me. While these incels were driven underground, with just a few clicks any of us normies can get onto an incel forum, and having spent a few days secretly hanging out in one we can confirm that it is a scary echo chamber of hate, rage, and the notion of genetic predeterminism. After reading the posts and discussions on a forum like incels.me, it's incredibly easy to see that these men hate women, they hate the world, and they hate themselves. They look at everything in life through the lens of intense hatred.

Basically, incels are unable to find a relationship or get laid and they violently loathe anyone who can. As far as they are concerned, the reason for their solo sex lives is partially due to attractive men who have sex with too many women and therefore monopolize the sex game—but of course, it's also all women's fault. Why? Let us explain.

The Socio-Sexual Hierarchy and Other Fun Stories

The socio-sexual hierarchy is a fun tier system of sexual desirability that incels have created. At the top of it sit the *alphas*, or *Chads*. In incel lingo, a Chad (or to give him his full name, Chad Thundercock—and no, we're not making this up) is the archetypal high-status male. As his full name suggests, Chad gets all the sex in the world. Physically, Chads are tall, attractive, muscled, and have strong chins (not unlike our dear Hannah); there is a lot of weak-chin obsession on these incel forums.

According to incels, Chads invariably treat women incredibly poorly, but us women are so simple and dumb that we fall for these men anyway. Incels see themselves as the nice guys or "supreme gentlemen," who are always overlooked by women because at heart all women just want hot, bad guys who treat them terribly. And apparently, when a femoid is in the presence of a Chad she experiences "gina tingles"—*gina* being a cute little incel term for a vagina. These tingles take over our female brains and stop us from thinking rationally.

For men with self-professed little to no experience with women, these incels sure seem to think they know an awful lot about vaginas . . . and their tingles. *(For starters, they don't even seem to know that the correct terminology here is not "gina tingles" but "fanny flutters.")*

On the next tier down from the Chads are the *betas*. These men are what incels would describe as sellouts. They aren't attractive enough or bad-boyish enough to get *all* the sex, but by giving in to the man-hating agenda of feminism, they do get *some*. Betas are often referred to as "cucks." What's a cuck? Well, it's a man who is desperate for acceptance, approval, and affection from women, but his desperation has led to the compromise of his true values and the desecration of his dignity and self-worth. Essentially, incels believe that (1) cucks are just pandering to women in order to get sex, and (2) that women should know their place, be dominated, and forced to have sex.

Interestingly, Dwayne "The Rock" Johnson and John Legend are named regularly on incels.me as cucks. It *appears* that this is because these celebs seem to respect and care about their wives. *(We've said it before and we'll say it again: someone get us a couple of cucks!)*

Speaking of finding ourselves a cuck, as we both creak into our thirties, incels would say we're already well over the hill, if not totally buried under it. Because in the mind of the incel, the sexual life cycle of the average woman goes a little something like this: Until the age of 25, women ride the "sex carousel," getting it on with as many alphas as we can. Then we eventually settle down with a well-trained beta we can keep in line. This is because, according to incels, femoids "hit the wall" at 25, after which point we become less and less sexually desirable.

Incels have also started borrowing a rather festive term coined by Japanese businessmen to describe women over a certain age—*Christmas cake*. According to Urban Dictionary, Christmas cake is meant to be eaten on December 25th; after that it's gone bad and it might as well go in the bin. *(Do you get this incredibly funny "high IQ" joke?)* So all you ladies out there, tick tock. Or, you know, find yourself a cuck who likes coagulated Christmas cake in April.

But anyway, back to the sex tiers. After the alphas and the betas come our boys the incels—or the *omegas*. According to incels, an omega is a low-status male who has no chance whatsoever of getting laid, at all, ever. Pickup artists, or PUAs, on the other hand (another creepy inhabitant of the manosphere swamp) also call themselves omegas, but they believe that they can use "the game"—a set of techniques designed to seduce and manipulate women—to overcome their lack of physical attractiveness. These surefire techniques that are guaranteed to win you sex and love with any woman include negging, harem management, premature intimacy, and kino escalation. If you're thinking WTF check out our sidebar for the gag-inducing details.

HATE THE "PLAYER" AND HATE THE GAME

PUAs are the absolute worst, and so we take great pleasure in writing this embarrassing list of their sad manipulation techniques. Once you know what these tricks look like, you'll spot the bullshit a mile off. Now don't get us wrong, these techniques are hardly a secret—they were clearly outlined by author Neil Strauss in his 2005 book *The Game: Penetrating the Secret Society of Pickup Artists*, but let's have a gander at some of the highlights.

Kino Escalation: This is the gradual invasion of a woman's physical space; PUAs will gradually escalate their physical touch to test the boundaries and see how far they can go.

Negging: A "neg" is a backhanded compliment designed and delivered to lower a woman's self-esteem and make her more eager to seek the PUA's validation.

Harem Management: PUAs will always bring up their exes or other women to manufacture love triangles, or false competition to make themselves look highly desirable.

Premature Intimacy: This tactic is to force a woman to be vulnerable quickly, and it usually involves the PUA proclaiming on the first date how emotionally invested and smitten he is.

So, as you can see, PUAs are just as misogynistic as incels; they are per-haps just a little bit more optimistic. Incels, however, have taken what they call "the black pill," and if you're thinking that sounds familiar and com-pletely unoriginal, you'd be right—it comes from *The Matrix*. In the world of incels, though, "taking the black pill" means waking up to the idea that the most important factors in attracting women are looks and physical traits *(because us women are shallow and stupid—and of course, no examples whatsoever exist in the real world of women being attracted to any men ever who aren't perfect Adonis-bodied thundercocks).*

Incels say that without certain physical traits, a man can never succeed with women and should therefore just give up. It is an idea based in biological determinism, total hopelessness, and sexual nihilism. Incels wear this griev-ance ideology like a protective exoskeleton. It gives them the freedom to say that they are just victims of circumstance; there is no point in their trying to work on themselves or to address why they might be struggling to make meaningful connections with other people. And it's common to actually see people on the internet sympathizing with these men because, yes, they are lonely and social isolation is a terrible thing. But hold up. As Jennifer Wright put it in a 2018 *Harper's Bazaar* article, "Their existence is not about being lonely. It is about blaming women for their loneliness."

Entitled

Incels are also all about entitlement. In her book, *Entitled*, author Kate Manne explains this really well: yes, incels complain about the fact that women will not have sex with them, but their real issue is often that they are not receiving the *right* kind of attention from the *right* kind of women. As you can see from their weird sex-ladder descriptions of men, incels see the world as a black-and-white hierarchy broken down into categories of people defined by their appearance and sexual status. In the world of men, these are the alphas, betas, and omegas. When it comes to women, they are either *Stacys* or *Beckys*.

A Stacy is the female counterpart of a Chad—a high-value woman who is attractive and desirable. Beckys are the opposite of Stacys—unattractive, usually flat-chested women. Incels want Stacys and feel angry that Stacys want Chads. Incels feel entitled to love, pleasure, and power and they don't want it from Beckys. But if a woman dares to desire pleasure and power, and that pleasure comes from a man she finds desirable, then she is of course a slut. To incels, her making that choice for herself is in itself not fair, because when she makes that choice it means that she is directly denying incels the pleasure they feel they are owed.

OK, OK, we get it—this is a weird one to wrap your head around, so let's consider the teen romances we all used to watch . . . The hot girl was an idiot because she didn't notice the geeky guy who *really* loved her; instead she wanted the hot jock. She was always horrible and mean to the geeky guy, but he *still* loved her. Why? Well, if she wasn't very nice to him, then he only liked her because she was hot. However, in the movie his love would be portrayed to the viewer as pure and wholesome. The hot girl not fancying him and liking the hot guy instead was presented as shallow and slutty, naturally.

Why is the geeky guy a sympathetic character despite his shallowness, but the hot girl is a bitch? This puerile worldview of men being "friend-zoned" or ignored by a woman they want, and then feeling victimized and resenting her for it, is the founding principle of the incel movement. The idea is completely interlinked with the notion that women cannot be trusted to decide who they want sexually; they are far too inferior to make decisions that in any way affect men. Left to their own devices, women will choose the dominant dickhead and ignore the gentleman in front of them: the incel *(who, as if it weren't already clear, is anything but a gentleman).*

The Road to Radicalization

By simply blaming their issues on something they feel is totally out of their control (their appearance), incels relieve themselves of any personal responsibility. It's all someone else's fault. This way of thinking is not unique to incels by any means, and in fact this deep-seated grievance is a fundamental commonality we see in those who are prone to any kind of radicalization across the board. Consider racists: if they aren't as success-ful in life as they'd like to be, immigrants and minorities must be to blame. When we consider these similarities (blaming or scapegoating others chief among them), it's easy to see why there's a definite dovetailing of extreme right-wing communities and incel communities online.

Pathetic as their ramblings are, don't be fooled. It's this hopelessness and grievance that make incels so dangerous and the most violent group within the manosphere. (PUAs believe that they can manipulate women into giving them what they want, and other groups like MGTOW—Men Going Their Own Way—have decided they don't want women at all because we are all a bunch of bloodsucking parasites.)

Incels *desire* love and sex, but they feel hopeless in getting them. And this hopelessness fills some men with what they call "omega rage," a point at which their total lack of sexual hope leads them to commit vio-lence, suicide, or murder. *So* much of incel ideology interlinks not just with the thinking of other extremist groups, but also fundamentally with terrorism. Many incels, just like Minassian, call for a "beta uprising" or the "incel rebellion," which refers to a mass uprising of all betas and omegas joined together to get revenge on all women and quash the rise of an oppressive dystopian feminist society. Retribution will be sought via violence against all women to force and scare them into "giving nice guys a chance."

This of course reinforces the idea at the heart of the incel philosophy—that women are expected to provide sex not because they want to, or because they feel attracted to the person, but because they *must* in order to please men. The group firmly believes there should be consequences to saying "no." If that's not terrorism, then what is?

Elliot Rodger, "The Supreme Gentleman"

In our opinion, no one paints a clearer picture of this ideology than the incel hero—Mr. Elliot Rodger, who was in fact the first individual to be labeled a terrorist of the alt-right by the Southern Poverty Law Center.

Rodger had been a ticking time bomb for a very long time. He posted YouTube videos and online rants about how he was filled with rage at the sight of "brutish men" with beautiful women who ignored him. "The supreme gentleman" Rodger also left behind a very, very detailed 141-page biographical manifesto called "My Twisted World." And yes, while it is a toe-curling, stomach-churning, wanting-to-scrub-the-eyes-with-bleach kind of read, his videos and manifesto do give us a pretty unique view into how Elliot Rodger went from weird teenager to mass murderer.

So, let's start at the beginning. Elliot Rodger was born in London in 1991, and at the age of six he moved with his family to LA. (The Rodgers were a pretty wealthy family—in all his videos, Elliot is wearing designer clothes and driving around in a BMW, even as a student. *Never trust a fucker who learned to drive in a fancy car.*)

Soon after the LA move, Rodger's parents split up. In his manifesto Rodger talks about how this destroyed his life. Clearly it had an extremely devastating impact on him, but although divorce can be difficult for kids to deal with, given that 50 percent of marriages in the US end this way, it's a pretty normal thing to happen. Rodger, however, writes about his parents' divorce as having *doomed* him.

His issues seem to have run deep right from the start. As a child and then as a teenager, Rodger struggled to engage with other people and the world around him. He wouldn't make eye contact, he barely spoke, and he was painfully socially awkward. He also seems to have been disconnected from the reality of his own behavior. In his manifesto he writes about continuously making an effort to meet and engage with women, but how he was constantly rejected.

This is a fundamental part of the incel belief system: that they fail with women despite *trying*. But for Elliot Rodger, and most incels, this is just part of their fantasy blame game. Because in reality Rodger had most likely never even had a conversation with a woman outside of his family—and not because stupid women are all attracted to abusive "brutes" rather than him, "the supreme gentleman," but because he wasn't good at speaking to women (or other people in general).

At this point, perhaps you feel some sympathy for him. Loneliness isn't a good feeling, and Rodger was clearly dealing with some serious unmanaged anxiety issues. But Rodger, like other incels, externalized all the rage he most likely felt toward himself and blamed his self-loathing on women instead. This blame then spiraled into radicalization and eventually violence. Reading his manifesto, we can see his preoccupation with the injustices he believes have been thrust upon him; like many mass murderers or spree killers, Elliot Rodger is what is known as an "injustice collector." He rants and raves about women, claiming, "It's an injustice, a crime, you ignore me and go after these obnoxious men when I am the supreme gentleman."

Elliot Rodger, although not the first incel to go on a killing spree, really has become not only a weird cult figure of reverence in this world, but also a blueprint for the archetypal incel killer. Like many in this space he totally immersed himself in an online echo chamber of hate, grievance, and misogyny. But we can also see, through his manifesto, the anticipation he felt toward starting college, calling it "a time when everyone has sex." It seems that he thought college was his chance to start fresh, but without having addressed his social anxiety challenges and with his ongoing obsession with online forums, things weren't any different after he joined the University of California, Santa Barbara in 2011.

There, Elliot Rodger began bubbling away with a white-hot rage. In 2012 he even bought a gun—a Glock 34 semiautomatic pistol—and he started writing in his diary about feeling a "new sense of power." He also found himself crossing more and more lines with people in real life. He raised several eyebrows on campus when he started throwing coffee at couples he saw, or at girls who rejected him, and he also started filming himself hiding and spying on couples. This kind of confrontational behavior and voyeurism *(similar to a man who says his favorite director is Quentin Tarantino)* is rarely indicative of anything good.

By the spring of 2013 Rodger was in therapy, at the request of his parents, but it wasn't doing much to quell his growing rage. In fact, at this point he was adding to his arsenal; he bought another handgun, the much more powerful SIG Sauer P226. After this purchase he wrote in his diary, "Who's the alpha male now, bitches?"

He also started to become more and more immersed in online forums like PUAhate and ForeverAlone. These forums were addictive to Rodger because they amplified and cemented his worldview, allowing him to find people just like him, who were angry about the same things he was, and who hated life as much as he did. These forums were the perfect echo chamber where violent thoughts and words became louder and more extreme. He was engaging in this hate on a daily basis, posting disturbing, aggressive, misogynistic, and racist messages. But even on these forums, where he was met with acceptance and even applauded, Rodger still couldn't connect with people. He claimed that although his new incel pals shared his hatred for women, unlike him they were too cowardly to act on it.

"The Day of Retribution"

Rodger was getting closer and closer to D-Day, but being the magnanimous young man he was, he wrote in his journal: "I will give the female gender one last chance to give me the pleasures I deserve from them." Again, this highlights the idea that women *owe* him sex and that women exist purely for their reproductive and sexual capabilities. If this was a one-off man thinking this, it might be easier to write off as merely a load of nonsense, but this philosophy was fundamental to the extremist communities on websites Rodger used daily, and as we'll see later in this chapter, hardly an isolated ideology.

So for this "one last chance," Rodger decided to try his luck with the ladies at a college party. But instead of wooing beautiful girls with his charm and supremely gentlemanly skills, he got blind drunk and ended up in a fight. On his way home a concerned neighbor spotted him and tried to help. According to this person, who stayed with him for hours, Rodger was incredibly emotional and barely spoke until he finally pulled himself together and said, "I'm going to kill all those motherfuckers, then kill myself."

On April 30, 2014, the police received a call from a mental health worker who had been contacted by Elliot Rodger's mom and dad, after they had watched a video he had posted to YouTube. The police went to Rodger's apartment but, unbelievably, he was able to talk his way out of it by claiming it was just a misunderstanding, and the police left. This would prove to be a huge mistake. Just three weeks later Elliot Rodger would go on his killing spree. If they had searched his place they would have found his angry manifesto and the guns.

On May 22, 2014, Elliot Rodger, then just 22 years old, uploaded another strange video to YouTube. It was called "Day of Retribution" and it featured the young man sitting in his car talking straight to the camera. This video is bizarre to say the least; in it, Rodger speaks in his characteristically calm, villain-esque tone explaining that tomorrow will be the day he gets his "revenge against humanity," and how he's going to punish everyone for "the blond stuck-up sluts who rejected him." This almost 15-minute-long video ends with Rodger telling the world, "I hate you. I hate all of you. I can't wait to give you exactly what you deserve—annihilation."

At around 9 p.m. the following day, Rodger emailed his manifesto to his parents and his psychologist. He then murdered his housemates, James Hong (age 20) and David Wang (age 20), and their friend George Chen (age 19), who was just staying over for the night. Rodger stabbed them all to death as they slept and wrote in his manifesto that he wanted to kill them so that he could turn their apartment into "his own personal killing and torture chamber."

After these senseless murders, Rodger started what he called his "war on women" and headed straight to the Alpha Phi sorority house. He arrived there at 9:25 p.m., carrying three semiautomatic weapons and hundreds of rounds of ammunition. He banged on the door of the house but no one answered. It was then that he saw three women outside—Veronika Weiss (age 19), Katherine Cooper (age 22), and Bianca de Kock (age 20)—and immediately opened fire. Heartbreakingly, Veronika and Katherine died on the spot, but Bianca, who was hit five times, somehow survived.

Rodger then headed to a place called the Ivy Deli; it was 9:30 p.m. and the place was packed. When he got there he started shooting into the shop. Inside, one of his bullets hit and killed 20-year-old student Christopher Michaels-Martinez. It's hard to know exactly what was going on in Rodger's mind at this point, but psychologists say that spree killers motivated by revenge always think that the rampage will make them feel better; it rarely does. So we can assume that at this stage in the game, Elliot could have been feeling frustrated that the release he was looking for just wasn't coming.

If you're wondering what the differences are between a spree killer, a serial killer, and a mass murderer, see the sidebar.

SPOT THE KILLER DIFFERENCE

Elliot Rodger is what we can call a spree killer. You may already know what we mean by that, but let's do a quick definition check-in.

A **serial killer** is relatively easy to define—it's someone who kills at least three people in separate and distinct incidents, with cooling off periods in between. A **mass murderer** is someone who is generally defined by a single event in which they kill four or more people. A **spree killer** is someone who kills two or more victims in a short time, in multiple locations, with almost no break between murders. Elliot Rodger could technically be called a spree killer or a mass murderer (there's a whole argument about this even in academic and law enforcement circles), but for our purposes we're going to say that he's a spree killer, because he covered quite a lot of ground to carry out his attacks in various different locations.

Despite his anger after the deli shooting, Rodger calmly got back into his car and started driving down the streets of Isla Vista, firing his guns at random. He opened fire on a group of students outside a 7-Eleven store, but by this point the police were there and firing back. One of the officers even managed to hit Rodger in the hip, but even this didn't stop him. Rodger likely knew he was in the endgame, and he had already planned for this. He wrote in his manifesto weeks before the attack, "When the police come I will speed away ramming and shooting as many people as I can until I find a suitable place to finally end my life."

Spree killers like Rodger want to cause absolute mayhem, and then they want to die quickly. This is so they can be martyred for their "cause"—and so they don't have to face the consequences of their actions. Like we said before, Alek Minassian, the Toronto van killer, tried to get the cops to shoot him, but luckily the arresting officer was able to bring him in alive.

Elliot Rodger wasn't going to take that risk, and just 12 minutes after he fired his first shot, he crashed into some parked cars and shot himself in the head. By the time he was finished he'd murdered six people and injured 13. The following morning, the police went to his apartment, where they found his manifesto and the bodies of his housemates. During Rodger's attack, his parents, who had received and read his manifesto just minutes before he started his spree, had been racing from LA to Isla Vista to stop him, but they did not get there in time.

As you can imagine, this horrendous shooting absolutely dominated the headlines at the time, but something notably missing from the news stories was the word *terrorist*. The media seemed much more keen to focus on Rodger's mental health issues rather than the ideology that had driven him to kill. The story was much the same when, four years later, Alek Minassian committed mass murder. Again, we did not see the media use the big T word, even though he and Rodger had both *explicitly* told us their motivations.

Most countries define terrorism, in a legal sense, in more or less the same way. The US Code of Federal Regulations defines terrorism as "the unlawful use of force and violence against persons or property to intimidate or coerce a government, the civilian population, or any segment thereof, in furtherance of political or social objectives." The UK's Crown Prosecution Service agrees; they state that terrorism is "the use or threat of action, designed to influence any government organization or to intimidate the public. It must also be for the purpose of advancing a political, religious, racial, or ideological cause."

As we've seen through our discussion of the incelosphere's sordid sexual hierarchies and their accompanying rage, incels don't just hate *individual* women. They have a clearly formed ideological and social cause for which they are fighting, and they are furious with society itself, raging at the whole damn system—a system that in their minds is keeping them and their dicks down.

Incels are filled with anger that society has moved, and is continuing to move, in a direction that increasingly allows women to make their own decisions about everything from work to sex and love. These men feel that this freedom afforded to women is directly oppressing *them*. Therefore, they believe, they have become a marginalized group within society and a violent revolution is needed in the shape of their "incel rebellion."

The Robin Hoods of Sex

At the heart of incel ideology lies the objectification and commodification of sex and women; one of the most prevalent talking points you'll come across if you ever visit an incel forum is the idea that women and sex should be *redistributed*—like a tax plan. Incels compare their sexual plight to that of the poor who are deprived of food, shelter, or other basic human rights; they argue that if money can be taken from the rich to help support these people through monetary redistribution and taxation, then it's only fair that all the women in the land be apportioned out to men by some sort of government-sanctioned girlfriend or wife program. *(We're not making this up—this is what they are talking about with absolute conviction and sincerity on their forums. We've seen it.)*

Basically, these incels claim that their virginity is a discrimination issue—some even compare it to apartheid and they are adamant that only a state-funded girlfriend distribution program, outlawing multiple partners, can rectify this grand injustice. *(Imagine how outraged they would be if they were on the other end of the gender pay gap or had essential healthcare products taxed as luxury items. The horror.)*

Militant Misogyny

Thankfully, it's not just us who think that violent incels are terrorists. The Anti-Defamation League in the US has been keeping an eye on incel groups for years, so sure are they that this community is a *serious* emerging domestic threat. The study "Recognizing the Violent Extremist Ideology of 'Incels'" by Shannon Zimmerman, Luisa Ryan, and David Duriesmith clearly highlights to us why laughing them off is the wrong way to think about incels. These men fit in perfectly on the spectrum of extremist groups we all already know—groups that may span a vast range of political ideologies, from white supremacists to the so-called Islamic State, but remain united by one thing: militant misogyny.

Terrifyingly, this is an ideology that is rapidly growing. Up until 2017 the Reddit forum r/incels had around 40,000 active members when it was banned that year. Unfortunately, this ban just drove the incels underground into fragmented forums. Now estimates place the incelosphere at around 100,000 members, and we would guess that this is probably a conservative estimate.

It's also not just the women-hating that these terror movements have in common, it's their sense of grievance. Amy Barnhorst, the vice chair of community psychiatry at the University of California, has studied mass shootings for years. According to her what ties many of these kinds of killers together is "the grievance, the entitlement, the envy of others, the feeling that they deserve something that the world is not giving them. And they are angry at others that they see are getting it."

This kind of hostility and feeling like the world is out to screw you can be linked to some mental health issues and personality disorders. So while mental health certainly plays a role in these attacks, focusing only on that factor (as we saw in the cases of Minassian, Rodger, and other incel attacks) just doesn't give us the full story.

Many of these violent incels have no interest in self-reflection; they don't sit down and think about *why* they may not be happy or thriving. And this isn't us just assuming this—remember, they themselves call for taking the black pill. This "self-acceptance" that they are sexually doomed no matter what they do acts as a shield for incels to avoid facing up to their issues or asking for help. Changing ideologies is much easier than changing yourself.

Since it is clear that what motivates incels is a distinct ideology—a hatred of women—and that they see it as a political issue, several questions arise. Why isn't this hatred taken more seriously as the reason behind these kinds of attacks? And why doesn't terrorism seem to be taken into account when it comes to sentencing these criminals? After all, if it were based on the crime being terror-related the sentence would most likely be far longer.

We think the reason it's hard for people, and even law enforcement, to see misogyny for the killer ideology it is is because of just how widespread and mainstream misogyny already is within our society. So even when we have men who actively go out to kill women—explicitly stating that they are doing so because of a political ideology they hold and for a social cause they believe in—we as a society still just look at these crimes as the separate acts of an individual and not as terrorism.

What's fascinating is that incels are by no means unique in this way of thinking; again, not only does misogyny already exist within every layer of our society, but consider for a moment how militant misogyny unites many *disparate* terror groups. Specifically, how all of them feel aggrieved by female empowerment and want not just a return to "traditional" gender roles but the total subjugation of women. The so-called Islamic State, neo-Nazis, incels, etc. all obsess over the purity of women and men's "right" to have unquestioned access to women's bodies. One thing that should be clear is that we must all call terrorism *terrorism* when we see it. We must also not sideline incels as if they are somehow inexpiable anomalies hiding in their mom's garages behind their computer screens. We cannot ignore that every single day around the world, countless women are killed for the exact same things incels cite as reasons to hate and even harm them. Women are killed for not being sexually available enough, but they are also killed for being "sluts."

We must call this dangerous movement terrorism. And we must also remember that incel numbers are growing at such an alarming rate because the ideology of misogyny is not a difficult one for a person to adopt. It doesn't require someone to sit down and read masses of ancient scripture, learn another language, or even change their lifestyle. It is a readily available way of thinking that tells lonely men seeking validation that *it's not their fault*. Incels are far from the only people to hate women; they are caricatures and the physical embodiment of the misogyny that pervades every layer of every society.

CULTS

Agriculture, Artillery, and a Ukiah Utopia

KILLING, AS WE HAVE SEEN, CAN MAKE A KILLER FEEL omnipotent. To take another's life, to watch the light leave their eyes, to know that in that moment you were powerful enough to choose whether another human being continued to exist or not—these are the things that go on in the twisted mind and disturbed morality of a killer. What could be mightier or more godlike?

Well, there are a few killers who think they have the answer to this particularly harrowing (if rhetorical) question. After all, doing depraved things to other people yourself is one thing, but imagine if you were able to convince *someone else* to kill, rape, or torture? What if you could, just with your words, charisma, and charm, manipulate someone into committing the most heinous of acts? And what if this person was relatively "normal"— an individual who, without your influence, would never have even thought to harm another human being?

What if you then took it to another level and were able to control the lives of an entire group of people? Wouldn't that be the ultimate power trip? At that point, wouldn't you be the absolute king of control? To this, the cult leader says hell yes.

In this chapter we're going to explore two types of killers: the killer cult members, those seemingly ordinary people who become murderers at the behest of a leader; and the cult leaders themselves, those who take the very fundamentals of what makes a killer tick—power and control—one step further by ensnaring hundreds, if not thousands, of people in their web of manipulation, coercion, and deviance.

This chapter is jam-packed full of complex questions. What are the mechanisms of cult formation? How does the leader take and keep control? Why don't cult members leave when fucking crazy shit starts to happen? We'll get to all of it, we promise, but let's begin with what makes the cult member tick. What motivates a person to leave behind their entire life and follow a stranger who demands total submission?

#Cultgoals

We should start off by clarifying one thing: People don't join cults thinking they are joining a cult. People join religious organizations, political movements, yoga groups, knitting circles, fermented juice cleanse gangs . . . Whatever it is, people are just looking to belong, to find their tribe, to identify a higher purpose.

We humans are very susceptible to someone offering us a definitive answer to life's big questions. We welcome the opportunity to feel like our lives have true meaning, like we're a part of something bigger than ourselves. Cult leaders instinctively understand this very human need, perhaps better than most. *(Except maybe the marketers behind Crossfit, Herbalife, and luxury yoga apparel . . .)*

The aspiring cult leader draws people in by promising them the impossible. They will pledge to solve everyone's problems; heal the sick; enlighten the ignorant; help the "normos" transcend to a higher plane of being. They can give you it all; you just have to hand over your faith *(and of course all your money and your life, too, but who's reading the fine print?).*

Successful cult leaders are highly manipulative and skilled profilers of human behavior. They know how to spot and attract the right kind of people for their purposes. Yet these purposes—while always centered on a narcissistic need for adoration, power, and control—do vary from leader to leader. Let's compare a few . . .

Aum Shinrikyo, Yoga for Terrorists

Not unlike religious leaders, cult leaders will often identify what's missing from a society and seek to fill that gap with their own teachings and beliefs. Take, for example, Japanese cult leader Shoko Asahara. In the 1980s he saw that Japan had been undergoing a huge transformation, spiritually speaking.

This change had started in the 1930s, when the prominent religions of Buddhism and native Shintoism were banned and replaced by State Shinto. State Shinto stuck to traditional Shinto beliefs but made one *crucial* change—the Japanese emperor was now considered a divine being. However, after those atomic bombs were dropped on Hiroshima and Nagasaki, this god-claim became hard for the emperor to continue to pull off. And so, when the emperor was forced to hand over his divine rights and step down from his God-on-earth position, Japan went into religious flux.

By the 1970s, Japan was booming economically and the Japanese people were ready for something new, so hundreds of new religious groups tried to muscle in and carve out a tasty slice of the holy pie—and of course, get their hands on all that delicious disposable income. According to David E. Kaplan and Andrew Marshall in their book *The Cult at the End of the World*, Shoko Asahara was no different. Though Asahara was personally motivated by other desires as well—like all cult leaders—he had a desperate need to feel important.

Asahara was born in 1955 into an extremely poor family. As a child, his sight deteriorated and as a teenager he was sent to a state school for blind children. It was there that Asahara realized his need, and ability, for commanding power and control over his peers. He was one of the few teenagers at his school who still had partial sight in one eye, and he used this to become an oppressive playground dictator and con man.

As he grew up, Asahara realized that by appealing to social outcasts, and by exploiting Japan's spiritual turbulence, he could infiltrate society. And he wasn't wrong. Using some nifty yoga tricks—like the earth-shattering "standing on one leg" technique to convince people he could levitate—Shoko Asahara turned a group of weirdos called the Immortal Mountain Wizard Association *(we're not kidding)* operating out of a rented yoga studio in Tokyo into Aum Shinrikyo—a doomsday cult that grew to over 40,000 followers worldwide and is estimated to have been worth $1 billion by the time Asahara was arrested.

Like many cult leaders, though, Asahara wasn't content with his legions of dedicated followers or even all the money—he had to escalate. After a failed attempt to gain political power, Asahara decided to get his revenge on the Japanese parliament by ringing in the very apocalypse he had spent years predicting, all with a little bioterrorism in the form of multiple sarin gas attacks in the mid-nineties. In total, Aum Shinrikyo killed 27 people, but some estimates state that as many as 6,000 people were injured. Eventually Shoko Asahara was caught and convicted. He was hanged by the state in 2018.

Asahara's motivations for creating Aum Shinrikyo were quite standard. He longed for attention and adoration. As we'll see, this is highly typical of cult leaders; they are generally profiled as narcissistic psychopaths who are obsessed with power. And since we've already talked about psychopaths in this book, it's worth taking a look at narcissists, and more specifically, narcissistic personality disorder (NPD). See the sidebar on page 118.

NARCISSISTIC PERSONALITY DISORDER (NPD)

We've all called someone a narcissist—whether it's that person who posts an embarrassing number of selfies, that friend who never asks you about your life but insists you listen to every second of their day, or the writer who is convinced their privileged suburban childhood was actually super hard and very worthy of its own screenplay/novel/epic poem. They may well all have narcissistic *tendencies*, but it doesn't mean they have NPD.

According to the *DSM-5*, there are nine traits associated with NPD. And like many other disorders, it exists on a spectrum. Individuals can be narcissistic to varying degrees. For a diagnosis of NPD, one would need to demonstrate at least five out of the nine traits below. Cult leaders are very likely to hit almost *all* of the traits and therefore score very highly indeed.

❶ Grandiose sense of self-importance

❷ Preoccupation with fantasies of unlimited success, power, brilliance, beauty, or ideal love

❸ Belief that they are special and unique and can only be understood by, or should associate with, other special or high-status people or institutions

❹ Need for excessive admiration

❺ Sense of entitlement

❻ Interpersonally exploitative behavior

- ⑦ Lack of empathy

- ⑧ Envy of others or a belief that others are envious of them

- ⑨ Demonstration of arrogant and haughty behaviors or attitudes

Cult leaders tend to be people who feel like outcasts in ordinary society, but they become convinced that this is just because they are special and misunderstood. They fervently believe that they are destined for much more than their current lot in life and that they are only ostracized because society is ignorant and jealous. So, they conclude that if the proles will not bow to their genius, then they have to create a world in which they will receive the godlike level of love, adulation, and attention they truly deserve. *(Or they start a podcast.)*

There can, however, also be *other* motivators sprinkled onto this sundae of self-importance. Some cult leaders are driven to create secretive sects in order to normalize their own perversions ...

The Children of God, Flirting for Fish

Let's consider, for example, the Children of God cult. Their founder and leader David Berg was a disturbed pedophile and sex offender. He knew that society would never accept his particular proclivities for sexual deviance, so he decided to forge his own society where his perversions would not only be normal, but *holy*. For someone like Berg, starting a cult was the perfect solution; he now had access to cult members' children. He took immense pleasure in transforming what "normal" was for his followers and reshaping it through the warped lens of his own evil.

It seems unbelievable, but Berg was able to successfully "reeducate" his followers into believing that "God was love and love was sex, so there should be no limits, regardless of age or relationship when it comes to sex." Berg used this key tenet—backed up with propagandistic material he churned out about incest and pedophilia—to actively encourage the members of the Children of God to sexually abuse minors, often even their own children. Most of the people who committed these atrocities within the cult had not previously shown *any* inclination toward pedophilia, but yet they were able to cross this horrific line because of David Berg.

The mechanisms and mentality of how and why cultists are able to reorder their thinking to *this* extent is something we'll come back to later in this chapter. For now, let's consider why so many cults have ended in mass murder.

Always Have an Endgame

Whether it's the Branch Davidians, Heaven's Gate, or Aum Shinrikyo, there is a definite pattern of cults spiraling into wanton destruction. This could be due to the leaders' instability and insatiable need for power, but potentially also because cults by their very nature are unsustainable.

Predictions of the end of the world, guarantees of grand enlightenment, or promises of escaping your human flesh cage and transcending into a cosmic light-being on another planet are simply untenable. A doomsday leader who keeps promising the end of the world, like Marshall Applewhite of Heaven's Gate, for example, has to at some point deliver. Sure, you can keep pushing the date of the apocalypse further and further back, but that gets embarrassing *(ask the Mormons)* and eventually *something* has to happen. There has to be an endgame.

And if it looks like the world *isn't* about to be destroyed in a fiery apocalypse, *or* that the aliens on the comet aren't about to drop by and pick you all up, the cult leader has to find another, more permanent solution. The narcissistic, psychopathic personality of a cult leader would never allow the cult's followers to simply walk away. The leader could never admit that maybe they were wrong. If the end of the cult-y road has been reached, well then, the only option is to go out with a bang. But cult leaders don't usually *start* cults with mass murder in mind, and they also don't always start from a place of normalizing deviancy. Cults, just like religions, can begin from a place of love and altruism before diving headfirst into something nightmarish.

And that brings us to the main man of this chapter, the Reverend Jim Jones: a person who was criminally responsible for the deaths of 909 people in the deadliest mass cult execution of all time—the massacre at *(the not-at-all narcissistically named)* Jonestown.

Jim Jones started his cult, Peoples Temple, with an admirable goal in mind. He claimed that he wanted to build a society in which all people, including people of color, would be treated as equals. Hearing such a message from a white man in the US in the sixties and seventies was a breath of fresh air, if not downright revolutionary, and that's why so many of those disillusioned by the level of racial segregation and lack of civil rights at the time flocked to Jones.

Many of you reading this book may be familiar with Jim Jones, Jonestown, and the Kool-Aid. Those of you who are *truly* hard-core will already also have muttered under your breath that it was in fact Flavor-Aid and *not* Kool-Aid *(don't worry, we know)*. But there's so much more to the story of Jonestown than first meets the eye, and in this chapter we're going to look at how one man can be found responsible for mass murder without ever having pulled a trigger, wielded a knife, or prepared a single cyanide-laced cocktail himself. Or how those who originally joined a group that preached peace, love, and racial equality ended up savagely killing their comrades and children in a promised land they had built with their own hands.

As with almost all cults, the story begins with the leader himself, because it's from his pathology that the rest of the group will be shaped.

Hell and Hot Takes with Reverend Jim Jones

Jim Jones was born in 1931 in Lynn, Indiana, and it's safe to say that he had a difficult start. His family was poor, like no-running-water poor. His dad was an alcoholic who had been destroyed by World War II, and his exhausted mother was forced to work around the clock through the Great Depression to support the family. This meant that little Jim was often left to fend for himself. It also meant that the young boy—who was starved of any meaningful attention or love from his own parents—sought it out from others around him.

Growing up in a tiny town, deep in the Midwest, Jones noticed quickly that it was the preachers who commanded the most adulation and author-ity. So from an early age, Jim Jones knew what he wanted to be when he grew up. He began to practice playing God and preacher with a fun little childhood game. We don't know what he called it, but it mainly consisted of him killing stray animals and then holding funerals for them in front of a bunch of his kid buddies.

Jones's eccentric childhood behavior didn't stop there. While the other kids argued over who got to be which allied soldier in their playground war games, awkwardly, little Jim *always* wanted to play Hitler. It seems that even as a child, Jim Jones was entranced by power and how much of it one single man could hold.

These little quirks of running around in an American schoolyard in the forties, pretending to be the Führer, unsurprisingly meant little Jimmy Jones was not very popular. For much of his childhood, he was an outcast who spent a lot of time on his own. But all that changed when a prepubescent Jones finally found faith and community at the local Pentecostal Church. Jones was barely a teenager when he started delivering rousing sermons to adoring crowds who hung on his every word. At last, he had found his niche. Given his talent as a charismatic and captivating preacher—and as a savvy organizer—by the age of 25 Jim Jones had already set up his very own church.

Slight sidetrack: One of our favorite things to do when we're research-ing a case is to find out what jobs killers had *before* they fell into a life of murderous crime. Dennis Rader (a.k.a. BTK) was an electronics tech-nician; John Wayne Gacy was a politician and he also worked the kids' parties as Pogo the clown; Bundy even worked the phones at a suicide helpline. But we have to admit that perhaps Jim Jones takes the biscuit for the weirdest job. Because before Jones was an evangelical preacher and cult leader, he was a door-to-door chimpanzee salesman. Yes, that's right—in the sixties and seventies in the USA you could buy actual chimps in pet shops, or apparently even on your doorstep. But anyway, back to Jones and his church.

After Jones got himself set up, success came thick and fast as his excit-ing message of radical, socialist Christianity took hold. It's amazing to think now that this man, in the 1950s, was able to garner a following in super conservative Indiana by preaching communism! But we have to understand that although generally speaking this kind of philosophy in the US at the time would have been considered abominable—*treacherous* even—more and more people were becoming disillusioned with capitalism.

After years of postwar consumerism packaged as patriotism, and with the war in Vietnam just kicking off, many people in the area were lost, poor, and tired. And in the absence of a prosperous American dream to believe in, these people *needed* something more. So Jim Jones told them what they wanted to hear—that the pursuit of material things was flawed; that no one should be poor; and if they were worried about being "commies" they shouldn't be, because Jesus himself had been a big old communist, too.

Jim Jones, like all successful cult leaders, had struck at the exact right time with the exact right message. That generation was looking for a different way of life. Some turned to LSD, some founded the American Atheist Society, others followed the Grateful Dead from coast to coast, and unfortunately, some found Jim Jones and the Peoples Temple.

According to Jeff Guinn in his book *The Road to Jonestown*, Jim Jones's particular brand of Pentecostal evangelicalism was formed by his upbringing, which mirrored that of many of his followers. His experiences of poverty made him a big fan of communism and his life as an outcast made him a fervent supporter of racial integration. In fact, Jim Jones's passion for civil rights was so intense that on one occasion, after his father refused to let his Black friend come over for dinner, he left and never spoke to his father again. At that time Indiana was a deeply segregated state and so Jones's rhetoric was refreshing—a white man telling Black people that they were equal and that he loved them? Now, that was different. *He* was different.

And as if preaching social justice, racial and class equality, and deseg-regation weren't enough, Jones was a natural showman. He had all the razzle-dazzle needed to woo the crowds (and open those wallets). Jones had studied superstar preachers of the past and learned what made the truly top dogs stand out. He knew what he needed to do—he needed to bring out the big guns. So, he started performing miracle healings! And boy, did that pull in the masses. Soon people were coming from all over to watch the Reverend Jim Jones give sight to the blind and help the paralyzed to walk—all while he spoke of a future built on equality and love.

It was all of course just a carefully crafted circus, because like all mag-ical "healings" it was total bollocks; those who were being "healed" were just planted stooges who put on great performances. But, hey, it worked.

Soon, thanks to Jones's electric personality and narcissistic charm, his congregants were so in love with him that they were willing to accept any and all of his teachings. Through all the trickery and healing magic manipulation, Jim Jones kept racial equality at the core of his principles. He also claimed to want to lead by example, so Jones adopted multiple chil-dren from various different racial backgrounds, building what he called his Rainbow Family. His adopted son, Jim Jones Junior *(come on, what else did you expect?)* was actually the first Black child to be adopted by a white fam-ily in Indiana state history.

Are We a Cult Yet?

As you can see, Jim Jones's vision of an egalitarian utopia didn't sound all that bad at first. And while, yes, he was definitely lying to his followers about being able to heal the sick, some might argue this was just a means to an end—and after all, healings and even *exorcisms* are still practiced widely by many mainstream religions all over the world to this day.

So when did the *real* exploitation start? Well, Jim Jones and the Peoples Temple started to ask for 20 percent of their followers' incomes. But again, one could argue that's not *unbelievably* unusual even for an ordinary, societally accepted religion. Also, socialism was Jim Jones's whole bag; everybody putting money into one big pot that could be used to help others was the entire vibe of the Peoples Temple. It also appears that in the beginning, Jim Jones did *indeed* use this money for good. He built homes for the elderly, fed the poor, and started up a drug rehabilitation program. *(Considering Jones's own hefty drug problem, in hindsight this is pretty ironic. He famously wore sunglasses all the time. This wasn't to look cool and mysterious, but rather to hide how incredibly fucked up his eyes were.)*

So after reading all this, maybe you're thinking: How could Jones have been a psychopath? He wasn't stealing all the money and he seemed to be genuinely helping people. Well, just because a narcissistic psychopath like Jones doesn't feel empathy, this doesn't mean that he doesn't know what he needs to do to reach his ultimate goal: adoration. Remember, psychopaths and narcissists are happy to do good, as long as their actions are rewarded with admiration, attention, and love. And if it had ended here, if this level of power and respect had been enough for Jones, well then, no harm, no foul. But of course, the story doesn't end happily ever after in Indiana.

The next stage of our journey into the story of Jim Jones and the Peoples Temple is to understand *when* they made the shift from operating within the parameters of a normal religion and crossed over into cult territory.

What Makes a Cult?

One of the fundamental questions we have to ask when we discuss cults is: What's the difference between a cult and a religion? To those of us who may have experienced a particularly dogmatic version of organized religion in our lives, it may seem like there is little difference. And yes, while certain characteristics *absolutely* sit in the overlapping center of the Venn diagram, there are of course also key differences.

But, firstly, what's the same? Both religions and cults expect their followers to:

* Accept certain supernatural beliefs.

* Venerate sacred symbols and ideology.

* Revere spiritual leaders.

* Adhere to a special set of laws and doctrines.

* Carry out specific rites, rituals, and ceremonies.

With so many similarities, we can see how confusion arises over where a religion ends and a cult begins. But there are vital differences: Cults usually have a living charismatic leader who becomes a living deity. And of course, being divine, this person can never be wrong, so questioning the leader (or their teachings) is completely unthinkable. Cultists must also submit fully to this figure, physically, spiritually, economically, and often even sexually.

Achieving this level of control over someone, let alone a group of someones, is not easy. The only way it can work is if the cult leader has first totally broken down a follower's ability to think critically. To do this, cults use a series of mind control techniques, including hypnosis, starvation, sleep deprivation, social isolation, and tightly restrictive rules. They also mini-mize their members' access to non-cult sources of information and flood their followers with masses of cult-generated propaganda. Cults will often even change followers' names and identities to totally separate them from who they were before and remove any connection that remains between them and the outside world.

To be further encouraged to sever their ties with outsiders, members of a cult are also told that the world is going to end or be convinced that everyone outside of their group is intensely evil, or in some fun cases, *both*. This creates a handy "us versus them" dynamic that the cult leader can use to their benefit. This one is particularly useful when it comes to underscoring the idea that the laws and morality of the outside world are meaningless.

Most of you reading this are probably thinking, "Pah, that would never happen to me, I'm far too smart to fall for that nonsense." Well, maybe, but cults are actually full of highly intelligent people who purposefully go after who they deem valuable members. Cults want people who are intelligent and motivated, those who will work hard and not worry about pesky little things like not getting enough sleep.

Think about those tech companies that now offer their employees "fun" sleep pods in the office. Sure, it may be a cool new workplace trend, but we can't help feeling that there is something a little sinister about the whole idea. Is it really a perk to help the workers chill out? Or are they there because they never want you to leave? I mean, why waste all that precious time you could be working going home to sleep? *Just stay here! Look at our lovely hammocks! Because work!*

In any case, you see our point—cults want the very best workers, those who are driven and who will work themselves into the ground with no clue about balance. And successfully recruiting attractive, smart, high achievers makes it easier to enchant even more members. Often this targeted recruitment by cults works because intelligent, deep-thinking people, who also long to make a positive contribution to the world, may feel like they are failing to do so on their own. This leaves them susceptible to someone "showing them the way." So it's important to understand that joining a cult and staying in a cult isn't about intelligence. It's about abuse, and anyone can fall victim to that.

Now that we all understand the tactics of cults a bit better, let's get back to the Peoples Temple and the exploitation that began to emerge. Despite some followers already handing over 20 percent of their incomes to Jim Jones, he soon started to tell them that if they really wanted to win favor, they should leave their jobs completely and serve him, God, and socialism full-time.

(Ding ding ding—cult bell!)

But even after quitting their jobs, some of Jones's followers *still* felt that it wasn't enough dedication, so they were delighted when the Peoples Temple suggested that they could also hand over *all* of their money and their houses, too, in exchange for a small allowance, food, clothes, and somewhere to sleep. And all that could be theirs for the low, low price of giving away all their worldly goods, working for 20 hours a day, and sleeping for just two hours a night. Bargain.

Food deprivation and sleep deprivation—along with economic abuse— are *key* to cult management. It stands to reason that a poor, tired, starving person is much more likely to go along with whatever crazy shit you tell them than someone who's had a square meal, eight solid hours of shut-eye, and still has a home left to escape to.

As his control over his followers grew, so did Jones's megalomania. In one of his most famous sermons, he threw a Bible across the room, and when he was not smote by almighty God for desecrating His holy text, Jones told his followers, "There is no heaven up there; we have to make heaven down here."

This is a *fascinating* moment on the road to Jonestown, because Jim Jones initially used Christianity and a God that people were already familiar with to draw people in; he told them that he had a direct connection with Jesus and God—a hotline to the big man—so they should respect and revere him. But soon Jones couldn't help himself, *he* needed to be the all-powerful one and usurp God himself, and so communist Jesus got bumped. And it worked. By this point, the congregation was growing and Jim Jones was powerful and famous; he decided that it was time to look beyond Indianapolis.

In 1965, Jim Jones decided to take his show on the road and moved his church to Ukiah, California. He said that he chose Ukiah because he was convinced that it was one of the few sites that could survive a nuclear attack. *Why* Ukiah would purportedly survive is a bit of a mystery, but it doesn't matter. Jones was playing on the contemporary societal fear of nuclear war, painting himself as the knower of top-secret atomic truths and *also* starting to hint at the end times. Many birds, one Ukiah-shaped stone.

A year after the Ukiah move there were about 80 followers in the Peoples Temple; by 1971 there were *thousands*. In a time long before TikTok, aggressive Facebook ads, or being Insta-famous, Jim Jones was the king of marketing. How did he do it? Well, he got himself a fleet of Greyhound buses, filled them up with a bunch of young, attractive devotees, and sent them off around the country, recruiting new members under the banner of socialism.

It was now that the communal-living fun really took off. Members lived together, ate together, and planted stuff together, and people of all shapes, sizes, and—crucially—races were welcomed with open arms. This sort of insular, together-all-the-time lifestyle is *crucial* for cults. Jim Jones couldn't have people going off on their own, *thinking*, and mixing with outsiders who might tell them that they sounded nuts. And also, if everyone is locked down in one place, it's much easier to keep an ear out for any voices of dissent from within.

Through the Peoples Temple, Jim Jones claimed to be doing what God, in his view, had never done: build heaven on earth. At this stage Jones fully broke with traditional Christianity, declaring that communism had been his goal all along. Cult leaders who use an *existing* religious framework like this only do so to make the transition period more palatable for followers. After the initial growth stage of the cult is complete, the leader will usually end up subverting the belief system to serve their own needs.

But whatever beliefs Jim Jones had, his PR expertise, unique showmanship, and polished marketing meant that even the politicians of time loved a bit of Jim. They all knew that if they just dropped the Reverend a line, Jones would guarantee a huge crowd of his followers would show up to their next fundraiser/rally/rodeo. This whole "rent-a-crowd from the Peoples Temple" system was instrumental in 1970s local government elections in San Francisco and was *also* a keystone of the cult's power grab of political influence. Don't believe us? Angela Davis and Harvey Milk are both on record saying that Jim Jones and the Peoples Temple were something to be "admired."

By this stage Jones wielded so much influence that there was absolutely no external oversight into what he and his people were up to on their commune, and everyone in power—including the politicians he hung out with—failed to notice the warning signs of what was really going on. As Jim Jones's fame and influence continued to grow, so did his ego, and it wasn't long before things at the Peoples Temple started to get weirder and weirder—and not just sleeping-on-mattresses-on-the-floor and working-outrageously-long-farm-hours weird.

For starters, Jones told his followers that he was the *only* truly hetero-sexual man on the planet, and that everyone else was secretly homosexual. In his book *The Road to Jonestown*, Jeff Guinn throws this particular statement made by Jones into question, by saying that most survivors of the cult knew "Jones had occasional sex with male followers, but never as often as he did with women." So while Jones completely banned sex outside of marriage for his followers, he happily carried on satisfying all his own sexual desires with whomever he wanted. (Time for another *Ding, ding, ding!* cult bell—and this time it's for sexual exploitation, which according to survivors, was absolutely rampant under Jones.)

But of course, as you would expect with Jim Jones, he didn't miss an opportunity to claim that his insatiable prediction for consensual and non-consensual sex with his followers was all for the *greater good*. Despite being very obviously bisexual, he claimed that he was in fact disgusted by sleeping with men and that he only did it to help them feel truly connected to him—the almighty big man.

Jones's control over his followers' sexuality stretched to the extent that he didn't even approve of sex within marriage for the purposes of reproduction. Instead, he preached that adoption was the only way forward. People who already had children were absolutely expected to bring them to the commune. Once there, the red flags started waving pretty fast, with parents forced to sign statements saying that they had molested their children. The Peoples Temple would then hold onto these "confessions" as collateral, you know, just in case anyone thought about leaving. *(Is it even worth dinging the bell again?)*

Along with isolation, fear, and intimidation—the usual cult tactics—Jim Jones also used a particularly maniacal method of manipulation to control his followers. Jones would speak openly about his obsession with the idea of people killing themselves, and also his deep concern that he'd be assassinated. Given his radical promotion of socialist ideals, it appears that Jones was convinced he was *just* as politically significant as Malcolm X and Dr. Martin Luther King Jr. He just needed everyone else to believe this, too. Because in the twisted mind of Jim Jones, for him to truly solidify his standing as a *radical* leader—one speaking the truth and being attacked by the capitalist system—someone had to have a pop at him.

In 1972, at a church picnic, it happened—Jim Jones was shot in the chest. This assassination attempt sent shockwaves through the Peoples Temple. Followers closed ranks—they viciously protected their persecuted leader, and *crucially*, they became terrified of the outside world. If you haven't already guessed, this convenient shooting—that allowed Jim Jones to consolidate yet *more* power—was actually a setup. Jones knew how his people would react, and he was right. But even with his hold over his followers cementing daily, Jones could never be accused of complacency. He wasn't about to relax, he needed to *keep* doubling down.

In the Peoples Temple, as in all cults, loyalty was of the utmost importance. In order to keep everyone in line and combat the risk of uprisings, Jones created a group within the cult called the Planning Commission. If these spies got so much as a whiff of someone even thinking about leaving the Temple, they would go straight to Jones. These suspected defectors would then be called out in front of the entire congregation, and quickly, these public shamings turned into public beatings, which were recorded on audiotape. In a particularly brutal incident, a congregant's newly pierced ears were ripped apart, and the whole time Jones can be heard in the background laughing wildly.

Followers' loyalty was also tested constantly in a variety of ways. Once, Jones gathered his closest confidants and hosted a little wine evening with them. After they had finished, he told them that they had all just drank poison; he wanted to see how they would react to "dying for the cause." Jones was obsessed with what he called "revolutionary suicide," and he wanted to root out anyone who didn't have the stomach for it. That time he was lying, but we all know where this is headed . . .

The Utopia: Guyana

In 1974, somewhat out of the blue, Jones suddenly claimed that the US wasn't ready for the Eden he had planned. He used some of the money he had been siphoning from his followers to buy a plot of land in the middle of the jungle in Guyana. To say this brand-new commune was remote would be a huge understatement; it was only accessible using a tiny jungle airstrip, or if you were feeling up to it, a 19-hour boat ride. But isolation is the name of the cult game and Jones told his followers that this land would become Jonestown—home of their new utopia.

Over the course of the next year, more and more members of the Temple were sent down to Guyana to help with construction. At first this migration was covert; members traveled from airports in different cities in groups of no more than three so as to not attract attention. But in 1977, when Jim Jones realized that he needed to get the fuck out of the US, the mass exodus began. The media were finally onto him after a group of former Temple members, led by Grace Stoen (who was the wife of Tim Stoen, a prominent cult member and Jones's former chief legal adviser), had gone to the press with their stories of sexual abuse, violence, kidnapping, and fraud.

We think it's safe to say that Jones saw this coming and that he knew that sooner or later he would need that jungle commune hideout far from the pesky, prying eyes of the American press. Jones managed to escape just in time; hours before the exposé hit the stands he was on his way to Guyana. Once there, Jones simply dismissed any negativity or pressure from the outside—be it from the press, cultists' family members, or government bodies—as pure jealousy. With this move to the jungle, those in the Peoples Temple became even more disconnected from the outside world, not just physically, but from any source of information that was not Jones himself.

With the congregation now in Guyana, Jonestown began in apparent earnest. It was dubbed the "Peoples Temple Agricultural Project" and it was filled with rainbows, smiles, and dancing, but there were of course also huge sinister speakers set up everywhere that would blast Jim Jones's apocalyptic warnings on a constant loop. These announcements would often run all night so that Jonestown members could "learn in their sleep."

By this point, Jones had a life-threatening addiction to prescription drugs. He had swollen up like an amphetamine-addled blimp, and his speeches were starting to sound slurred. If anyone had any issues understanding him, though, it was OK because the Red Brigade—who were essentially the Planning Commission, but now with added guns—were there to help clarify things. And there's nothing like a gun in your face to sharpen your comprehension skills.

But there were other issues starting to emerge. Jonestown, which was now home to almost a thousand people, had been built to support *just* four hundred people. The much-lauded agricultural project had also been a total failure, so food was rapidly running out. And in another twist of stupidity, what food was being produced wasn't even being stored properly, and in the damp jungle climate the meager rations constantly got moldy.

The members of the Temple had always been hungry, but things were especially bad now. They were fed a tiny bowl of rice with milk, water, and a bit of brown sugar at 6 a.m. and that was it. With nothing more to fuel them, they had to spend at least 10 grueling hours working in the fields under the beating tropical sun. Anyone who complained would be reported straight to Jones himself—and given the growing viciousness of the public shamings, this made for some very compliant congregants indeed.

With these starving "zombies" stuck in the middle of a jungle in Guyana, too hungry, too scared, and too trapped to disobey him, we suspect that Jones perhaps started to feel somewhat dissatisfied. Maybe the thrill of the chase was over, or the shine from the control he had had worn off. As with other killers we have discussed so far in this book, dangerous people tend to continue to escalate their behaviors in order to get the same rush, so yet again, Jim Jones turned the abuse dial to an 11.

Jones started conducting a ritual called Peoples Forum three times a week. These events were an opportunity for congregants to show Jones how loyal and obedient they were, but of course, they were never able to keep him happy for long. Soon Peoples Forum nights would often turn into gladiatorial battles with violent confrontations and beatings. It was also during these public meetings that Jones would encourage/force his congregation to confess their deepest, darkest sins to him; again, like the signed child abuse "confessions," these secrets would be saved and used later if needed.

Despite the danger and all the threats, some members did try to escape, but most of the time they were quickly caught by the armed guards and taken off to the "extra care unit," where they were drugged and would usually only emerge weeks later, unable to speak. Incidents like these, although quickly "managed," made Jones increasingly paranoid. He still hadn't forgotten about the group of defectors who had gone to the press and denounced him back in the States. And they hadn't forgotten about him, either—in fact the group of whistleblowers had actually grown in size.

Back in the US, the families of those in Guyana had banded together through their collective grief and fear. They were terrified because they couldn't communicate with their loved ones at all and any miraculous letters that did arrive seemed highly censored and manipulated. Ex-members of the Temple were also starting to take notice; they knew exactly what Jim Jones was capable of, so they knew they had to ring the alarm.

Finally, after a great deal of lobbying and letter writing, the Federal Communications Commission in the US launched an investigation into Jonestown and its illustrious leader. The news reached Jim Jones through Angela Davis and other Black Panthers, who confirmed to the panicking cult leader that there was a "profound conspiracy against him." This was an existential threat of epic proportions for Jones, and he needed to take radical action. So he kicked off a trial run of a six-night siege! That's right— the thousand starving and brutalized members of the Peoples Temple were forced to do a week of apocalyptic role-play in preparation for some sort of invasion. It was during this live-action horror show that the Peoples Temple started its routine of infamous "white nights," where members would practice committing mass suicide.

What we have to understand is that these "white nights" were the absolute pinnacle of Jones's ideology—if they couldn't live the way they wanted, then they wouldn't live at all. As we saw earlier, Jones was obsessed with "dying for the cause." He framed this as an act of protest he called "revolutionary suicide." Anyone who wasn't ready to die was a coward and a traitor.

Eventually, by the tail end of 1978, Congressman Leo Ryan agreed to take a delegation down to Guyana and meet Jim Jones to find out exactly what was going on down there. Ryan, his team, and some journalists arrived on November 17 and were met with a celebratory reception. Ryan was then given a tour of the impressive—if a little spartan—Jonestown Agricultural Project. All the Peoples Temple members even lined up to tell Ryan how very happy they were in the jungle.

That evening everyone gathered in the pavilion where they ate, drank, and made merry, although Jonestown survivors now say that there was a palpable tension in the air. This tension was broken, however, when Congressman Ryan stood up and said that he had been sent to find out about Jonestown and that "whatever the comments [back home] are, there are some people here who believe that this is the best thing to have happened in their whole lives." This statement was met with thunderous applause.

Despite all the clapping, some members of Jonestown *did* want to get out, and one of them was a man named Vern Gosney. Gosney knew this might be his only chance, so he wrote a note asking for help and gave it to someone in Congressman Ryan's group. Thankfully the team agreed to take Gosney with them, but they didn't seem to understand the grave danger of what was happening. In fact, one of the journalists, Don Harris, NBC correspondent *(and nominee for the Worst Decision Award 1978)*, so *massively* misread the severity of the situation that he actually handed the note to Jim Jones on camera and asked him why people were being held in Jonestown against their will!

A visibly startled Jones told Harris that this was all just a bunch of nonsense, and that anyone who wanted to go was free to do so. Following this revelation news quickly spread across the commune that Gosney was leaving on the plane with Congressman Ryan and his team, and it didn't take long for others desperate to get the hell out of there to pipe up, too. Soon the number of those wanting to flee grew to more than 20.

In her book *A Thousand Lives*, Julia Scheeres notes that Jones was furious, but he knew that the way to get them all back on his side was to plead with his flock like a dejected child. Just like in an abusive relationship, the apology was just a manipulative tool used by the aggressor to pressure the victim into forgiveness—and it worked. Upon seeing Jones look a bit sad, the most heavily indoctrinated cultists started to do what they'd been trained to: protect Jones and the "heaven" he was building.

Then suddenly, in a wild act of desperation, one of Jones's most loyal followers pulled a knife on Congressman Ryan. Clearly, realizing that they needed to get the fuck out of there as fast as humanly possible, Congressman Ryan, his team, and those he was taking with him made a break for it. An extra plane had been ordered for the escapees, and those brave enough to leave clambered into a truck and headed to the airstrip. But Jones wasn't going to make things that easy. The hopeful escapees were horrified, but probably not shocked, to see a tractor pulling a wagon full of eight of Jones's staunchest supporters hot on their tail.

Even from a distance it was clear to see that these men were armed to the teeth, and within moments the cultists in the wagon opened fire. In the shootout that followed, five people were killed, including the congressman. Back in Jonestown, a crisis meeting was already underway with Jones using what had just happened as fuel for his raging paranoia fire. He told the remaining residents of Jonestown that this was proof that the US government would never allow them to be happy; they just wanted to drag them all back to the capitalist nightmare of America and torture their children. It was very much a let's-chuck-it-all-at-the-wall-and-see-what-sticks kind of message, but it worked. *Again.* Resolutely, Jim Jones told his frightened congregation that there was only one way out. "If we can't live in peace, we will die in peace."

The End

We know more about the last hours of Jonestown than we do about any other cult, because Jones, ever the narcissist, was obsessed with recording everything. From the early days of his parish meetings in Indiana to the Peoples Forum get-togethers in Guyana, Jones recorded it all. Horrifyingly, we know exactly what happened next to those one thousand people. The recording of their final moments would go on to become known as "the death tape."

It's important to note that while Jones set in motion the final plan as a reaction to a catastrophic incident *(I mean, they'd just murdered a US congressman!)*, nothing about the shitshow that was about to go down had been left to chance. The fact that there was enough cyanide to kill one thousand people already at Jonestown tells us that this had been Jones's exit strategy for quite some time. It's also worth mentioning that although Jones was in huge trouble, it's highly likely that it never would have crossed his mind to turn himself in and deal with the consequences, or even to go on the run. Jones wouldn't have been able to bear people finding out what a failure Jonestown had been.

Much like with the classic psychology of a narcissistic family annihilator, as described by Elizabeth Yardley, David Wilson, and Adam Lynes in their 2013 paper "A Taxonomy of Male British Family Annihilators," Jones may have rationalized to himself that it was kinder to just kill his "family" than allow them to suffer on without him.

So, the cyanide was mixed with the Flavor-Aid, and Jones told his flock that their deaths would be painless and that there was no reason for them to be afraid. After this, the children were killed first, partly because they needed to be fed the poison and partly because once they were dead their parents were less likely to feel a need to live. Hundreds of tumblers of Flavor-Aid laced with cyanide were handed out to the children, and the babies who couldn't quite hold a cup yet had it injected into their mouths.

Cyanide had a reputation for being a quick and painless way to go because of its rise to fame as the suicide pill of choice in WWII, but we now know that it certainly is not. Cyanide will take between two to five minutes to kill you, and during that time you are fully conscious and unable to breathe until you enter cardiac arrest. Hundreds of parents had to watch their children's mouths fill with blood and vomit as Jones's voice poured over the PA system telling them that they needed to die with respect.

After the last of the children were gone, the adults were next. Some were all too eager to end things, but we also know that not all of them willingly drank the cyanide. Some bodies were later found with abscesses where the concoction had been forcibly injected into them. As his followers collapsed to the ground writhing and convulsing in pain, Jones intoned over the jungle sound system: "How very much I've tried to give you a good life . . . but in spite of all I've tried, a handful of our people with their lies have made our lives impossible. No man takes my life from me, I lay my life down. If we can't live in peace let us die in peace."

Eventually the Guyanese army, realizing that something was very wrong, sent a group of helicopters to Jonestown. The smell of decomposing bodies on the floor of the jungle made it all the way up to the helicopters hovering hundreds of feet above. On the ground the army found 909 bodies scattered across the compound; chillingly, some of the corpses had been lined up in rows, like someone had been tidying up in the middle of the massacre. Of the almost one thousand bodies they found, three hundred were never identified; most of them were children.

Jones himself was discovered with a gunshot wound to the head—he had not taken the cyanide. Maybe after seeing just how "painless" it was, he didn't fancy it for himself, but he knew he couldn't leave Jonestown alive. Like he had said to his followers so many times, the only way out of Jonestown was in a box.

When news of what had been found deep in the Guyanese jungle leaked, it shook the world. Up until the events of September 11, 2001, the massacre at Jonestown was the largest modern-day instance of intentional civilian death in the history of the United States. But amidst all the death and destruction, we're happy to say that there were survivors, too; some had run off into the jungle and some had managed to slip away when Jones had instructed them to take suitcases containing $7.3 million to the nearest Soviet Union embassy. *(It looks like Jones did have the money to feed his people after all . . . so much for the socialism.)*

AN UNEXPECTED VICTIM . . .

While most people know about the horrors of the human deaths at Jonestown, people rarely talk about the single chimp fatality. Remember Jones's previous life as a door-to-door chimpanzee salesman? Well, a fully grown adult chimp called Mr. Muggs lived with Jim Jones in Jonestown. Jones told everyone that he had single-handedly rescued Mr. Muggs from scientific experimentation, but it's much more likely that he had just bought him from a pet shop. Mr. Muggs's body was found in the jungle commune, too, but he hadn't been forced to take cyanide; he, like Jones, had been shot in the head.

Leaving Ain't Easy

We've tackled a lot of questions in this chapter, but let's come back to the key one that usually dominates the discourse around cults. Why did people stay even when everything was going so batshit fucking crazy?

There were, of course, a bunch of very real and very huge barriers to leaving the Peoples Temple. Remember that Jonestown was in the middle of the jungle in Guyana! So even if you managed to get to the airstrip—with no phone, no money, and no passport—how were you supposed to charter a plane to come get you, or pay someone to take you on the 19-hour boat trip back to civilization? This was a *huge* impediment, but there were other invisible ones, too.

Jim Jones used all the tactics we discussed on pages 127–129 and he was supremely good at almost all of them. The people in Jonestown were severely malnourished and they barely slept, which made decision-making and critical thinking difficult, if not impossible. And by isolating his followers, both geographically and ideologically, Jones was able to totally control the communication within the cult; not just *between* followers but inside the cultists' own heads.

Through the use of the Red Brigade, his Peoples Forums, and the public beatings, Jones also managed to sow a culture of extreme fear. The members of the cult were terrified of being reported for dissent so no one spoke to anyone about anything of substance. Being trapped, scared, and unable to communicate is of course a recipe for major anxiety and depression. Anxious, depressed people—who are scared out of their minds—are less likely to make elaborate escape plans. And they are much more likely to exhibit drastically changed behaviors, and even to kill themselves—whether it's under the guise of a revolutionary act or not.

Humans are emotional, and often behave irrationally. People will keep playing the lottery even though they know that the chances of them winning are slim to none. *Hannah will keep swiping on Hinge even though she knows she will die alone. Hope* is the key factor and we need it to survive. Hope is incredibly powerful stuff, and the people of Jonestown had loads of it; they *truly* believed that they were building a better world. And this brings us back to why cults go after intelligent, socially conscious, hard-working people—they are filled with hopes and dreams. And the followers of the Peoples Temple had attached such hope and emotion to Jonestown—and the racial integration and equality it represented—that they held onto it, come what may.

So why then did all of these normal people, fighting for a better world, kill themselves and each other? Jim Jones didn't trick them with secret concoctions; people knowingly poisoned their peers and their families. They did what they were told because they were broken people. Jim Jones had broken them. But what can explain this mental pivot on a deeper psychological level?

Well, there is a theory that being in a cult can cause people to exhibit borderline personality organization, which is one of the symptoms of borderline personality disorder or BPD.

WHAT IS BORDERLINE PERSONALITY DISORDER?

Borderline personality disorder (or emotionally unstable personality disorder) can happen for lots of different reasons, some genetic and some environmental. Often people with BPD have experienced a traumatic childhood. According to the UK's National Health Service and the charity MIND, those living with BPD feel emotions more strongly and uncontrollably than other people and exhibit disturbed patterns of thinking. Here are some of the symptoms:

* Intense fear of abandonment, but also being convinced everyone is going to abandon you even if you do everything right

* Extremely intense emotions that can change rapidly

* No strong sense of self-identity, meaning you can become very different around different groups of people and are easily influenced

* Feeling of emptiness

* Impulsive behavior that puts you and those around you in danger

* Self-harm

* Suicidal ideation

* Uncontrollable anger

* Extreme difficulty maintaining balanced relationships

* Paranoia

* Dissociation

Not everyone diagnosed with BPD will experience all of these symptoms, but generally more than seven of these, as outlined in the *DSM-5*, is considered to be enough for a diagnosis.

Life with BPD is a life of extremes and disturbed thinking. Suicidal ideation is a result of disturbed thinking, and the different forms this can take are laid out by David Lester in his paper "The Role of Irrational Thinking in Suicidal Behavior." Evolutionarily speaking, we are hardwired to want to survive, and so to end our lives is not rational behavior.

So why are we bringing all this up? Well, in the paper "An Object Relations Approach to Cult Membership," Joseph D. Salande and David R. Perkins argue that the repetitive activity, lack of sleep, and constant pressure to conform that cult members are often exposed to can actually cause their personality organization to break down to the point that their thinking resembles someone with borderline personality disorder, narcissistic personality disorder, or antisocial personality disorder.

And it does make sense—being indoctrinated into a cult is a traumatic experience and *everything* about a cult is built to weaken our normal functioning egos, induce dissociation, and compromise critical thinking. Now, these academics are not suggesting that cult members spontaneously sprout personality disorders. Rather, it's that cult experiences weaken a healthy person *so* much so that it causes the self-destructive behavior one might observe in someone with a serious personality disorder.

So, as unbelievable as what the followers of Jim Jones did may seem—biologically and psychologically—it would appear that a lot of people would act the same way, had they been put through what happened in Jonestown.

6
RELATIONSHIPS
Hormones, Hybristophilia, and Horse-Drawn Carriages

LOVE IS ONE OF THE MOST PROFOUND EMOTIONS THAT WE AS humans experience. It has the power to transform our lives, influence our mental health, and even affect our physical wellbeing. *(It can also absolutely ruin your life.)* The people we meet and the relationships we forge shape who we are. They have as much potential to determine our futures as our childhoods, our socioeconomic situation, or at what age we learned how to stop over-plucking our eyebrows.

Every rom-com, every song, and every annoying article that pops up on our Facebook timelines announcing "10 Signs to Know You've Found the One" tell us that love can change us for the *better*. And apparently, it's not just *us*. It seems that love can even help vicious serial killers.

Consider, for example, Gary Ridgway (a.k.a. the Green River Killer), whom we met briefly in chapter 2. He was one of the most prolific serial killers *ever*, having murdered up to 90 women over the course of a decade. During the peak of his killings, he had twice been unhappily married, but when he met a woman named Judith Mawson, fell in love, and married her in 1988, the murders essentially *stopped*.

It seems that some serial killers *can* stop, given the right circumstances—like a stabilizing marriage or reduced stress—and love can play a huge role in that. As criminologist Dr. Michael Stone put it in an interview with the *New York Times* in 2018, "Some of these men have little oases of compassion, within the vast desert of their contempt and hatred of women."

But what about a love that, instead of quenching a killer's drive to murder, actually feeds into it? Surely it stands to reason that if love can have *such* a powerful impact on a serial killer that it can stop them from killing, the pendulum can also swing the other way and make them even more brutal.

In this chapter, we're going to look at a case that we feel highlights this nightmarish match-made-in-hell situation perfectly so that we can examine how and why a romantic union influences murderous behavior. We'll also explore what drives those who may *never* have become killers had they not met that "right" person . . . who steered their lives into a big old murder ditch.

Killer Couples: Swipe the Fuck Away From Me

There's an image conjured up in all our minds when we think of a killer, particularly a serial killer—it's the idea of a lone man out stalking his victims, usually wearing a trench coat. We also know that most serial killers prefer to work alone; they have a specific MO, a fine-tuned set of motivations, and their own very niche fantasies. They don't want to share the thrill, and of course, many serial killers are not the most social of butterflies.

So this makes it all the more interesting when we *do* come across killer couples. But just how rare or common are they? In his 2002 book, *Serial Murderers and Their Victims*, Eric W. Hickey finds that roughly a quarter of serial killers actually operated as pairs or teams, and this number went up to almost a third when *only* female serial killers were analyzed. So while they aren't as common as the solo killer, couples or teams do make up a significant subset of this dangerous population.

What's *more* interesting, though, is the difference in dynamic. Studies show there are significant differences between solo and partnered killers in terms of number of victims, length of career, method of murder, and their motives. Generally, couples who kill together murder more victims, they are usually more brutal (thanks to the multiplying of motives when more than one person is involved), and they typically get caught faster. And while killer couples come in all shapes, sizes, and sexual orientations, in this particular chapter we're going to focus on the heterosexual killer couple, because the role of the woman within these unions—and the idea of female criminality itself—is so often massively overlooked. Typical.

This bias may well be because of who is perceived to be the more dominant partner—and therefore, more culpable. In 2015, Hickey analyzed the data pertaining to hundreds of serial killer couples and teams, and he found that in every example one person was in control. And this makes sense—in most relationships there is usually a more dominant partner. In these killer teams, it was usually the male, but the role of the female killer and her motivations are still vital to explore and understand. All too often, any theories that we *do* see thrown about as to why submissive women kill with dominant men completely dissolve the woman's agency.

The female in the pair is usually portrayed as just a weak-minded follower or a compliant victim, and sometimes that's true. *But* it is absolutely not always the case. Some women are *actively and happily* involved, driven by their own murderous and deviant desires. Just being the more submissive member of the pair doesn't mean that they were being forced or manipulated to kill. And while these submissives may never have killed before their murderous relationship, their darkest impulses are unlocked and unleashed by the dominant aggressor and they *fully* embrace it.

In such cases the two lovebirds sense something in the other, a dark kindred spirit. This draws them together and they become bound by the emotional glue of shared dysfunction, abuse, and chaos. This can create a powerful "us-against-the-rest-of-the-world" mentality and allows the couple to romanticize themselves as Bonnie and Clyde–like antiheroes. And although Jay-Z and Beyoncé's *'03 Bonnie and Clyde* is an absolute banger, we won't be doing any romanticizing in this chapter, because let's not forget Bonnie and Clyde killed at least 13 people.

So let's get started with the main characters at the center of this chapter: Karla Homolka and Paul Bernardo.

The Ken and Barbie Killers

Karla Homolka and Paul Bernardo—a couple who brutally tortured, raped, and murdered three girls together—got the rather perky moniker of the "Ken and Barbie Killers" thanks to their good looks. Karla was a fun, outgoing, blonde teenage girl and Paul was a tall, handsome man oozing confidence and charisma. The nickname, although annoyingly glamorizing, is perhaps fitting because their appearances *did* play a key role in attracting them to each other, and also possibly in helping them fly under the radar for as long as they did. But before we get to their whirlwind romance of death, let's start with who Karla was pre-Paul.

KARLA

Karla grew up in Ontario, Canada, the eldest of three girls in a loving and supportive family. As a child, Karla had been a bit difficult, described by some as being quite domineering, stubborn, and not playing well with others. According to the book *Karla: A Pact with the Devil* by Stephen Williams, she'd also been a bit of a bully at school, and displayed other signs of callous and problematic behavior. For example, she once threw a friend's pet hamster out a window with a homemade parachute strapped to its back. Sure, these things can happen when children are playing, but the hamster died and Karla didn't seem at all bothered.

We'll come back to Karla's specific personality issues and psychological makeup later in this chapter, but if there were any concerns about her at this point, they dissipated by the time she hit adolescence. Other than being prone to raging arguments with her parents, teenage Karla was popular, smart, and pretty *(even with the painfully 1980s bleach-blonde mullet/ bangs thing she had going on)*, and so as far as anyone who knew her was concerned, she was "perfect."

During her senior year of high school, Karla, while trying to figure out what she wanted to do with the rest of her life, got a part-time job at a local veterinarian clinic. This made her realize her passion for working with animals *(thankfully minus the parachute experiments)*. In October 1987, 17-year-old Karla Homolka headed to Toronto to attend a pet convention. It was there that she first laid eyes on 23-year-old Paul Bernardo.

Paul swaggered into the hotel bar, and for Karla, it was love at first sight. He had everything she wanted: he was older, he was charming, and to her, he was drop-dead bloody gorgeous. But there was much more to Paul than met the eye; there was a darkness in him bubbling away just beneath his perfectly coiffed Patrick Bateman hair.

PAUL

While Karla had been relatively normal up until the point that the pair crossed paths, the same can't be said for Paul. He *had* had a wealthy suburban upbringing, but it had been far from stable or happy.

The Bernardo home was a nightmarish one, and Paul's childhood traumas can be listed like a bingo card for predicting a future serial killer. First, Paul's father was extremely emotionally and physically abusive toward his mother and it was also rumored that he sexually abused Paul's sister. Kenneth Bernardo was actually convicted of child molestation in 1975, and as an adult, his daughter even pressed charges against him for the abuse she said she endured at his hands. Despite his turbulent home life, however, Paul was known for being a happy child and it wasn't until he was a teenager that a darker side of him began to emerge. The catalyst for this seems to have been that, at the age of 16, Paul discovered that his dad, Kenneth, wasn't actually his biological father, and that he had been conceived after his mother had an affair. This shook Paul's sense of self and he resented his mother for it. Discovery of true parentage can rock the foundations of a child's psyche; Ted Bundy, for example, claimed that a huge turning point in his life was when he discovered that his sister was actually his mother.

Of course, the negative impact of such revelations can be mitigated by parents who handle it in a kind and compassionate way, but considering the fact that Paul's parents started referring to him as the "bastard child from hell," we're going to say that they failed, quite considerably, on that front. As a result, Paul's fury toward his mother became explosive, and he would regularly scream at her, calling her a "whore" and a "slut." This anger grew into a deep sense of rage that soon spilled over into how young Paul viewed *all* women.

As an adolescent, he quickly became a voracious consumer of extreme pornography. By the time he was in college, Paul Bernardo was having violent fantasies about rape and dreaming about building his own "virgin farm" where he would keep women as sex slaves. As we said, Paul was an attractive guy *(if you like the preppy look)*, so he never had trouble finding girlfriends. Keeping them, however, proved to be less easy. Paul was obsessed with aggressive, degrading, controlling sex, and early into his relationships he would start to pressure partners into participating in sex acts involving bondage, asphyxiation, sodomy, and humiliation. The women he dated were just not into it, and they all ran the hell away.

In 1986, after months of harassment from Paul, two of his ex-girlfriends actually filed restraining orders against him. This incident appears to have been a trigger for Paul; it was soon after in May 1987 at the age of 22 that he committed his first known rape. By the time Paul met Karla in that hotel bar in October 1987, he had already raped two women and attacked a third.

Love at First Pet Convention

Within hours of meeting, Karla and Paul had ditched their friends and were in a hotel room having sex. As described by Nick Pron in his 1995 book, *Lethal Marriage,* after this encounter their relationship moved at breakneck speed. Paul, who by this point had graduated from college and landed a job with PwC, would drive from Toronto to Ontario every weekend to be with Karla. At first, Paul spoiled his teenage lover; he would shower her with affection, attention, and gifts. And Karla was smitten—Paul was everything she'd ever dreamed of.

But of course, it wouldn't last, and those of you who have been in a similar situation (*we both definitely have*) probably know what we're about to say next. Paul was using the narcissist's favorite power play: love bombing.

A favorite of the pickup artists we had the displeasure of meeting in chapter 4 and our ex-boyfriends, love bombing is a manipulation method used in particular by people with narcissistic traits. It's a way to gain and maintain control over another person. There are usually two phases to love bombing: the idealization phase and the devaluation phase. During the first phase, the target gets all the love, praise, and promises of a beautiful future together that they could hope for. But soon they find themselves in the devaluation phase, where the put-downs and the criticisms come thick and fast.

When Paul started to tell Karla that she was ugly and stupid, she was shocked. But now, being "addicted" to Paul and his love, Karla would do anything to please him and get back to that idealization phase. So the more

Paul devalued her, the more dependent Karla grew on him and the more desperate she became.

Paul began to introduce Karla to more of his extreme fantasies, and the pair began to engage in some pretty hardcore BDSM—with Karla assuming the role of slave to Paul's master. Of course, an interest in BDSM doesn't make you dangerous; *consensual* BDSM—just like *consensual* missionary— is totally fine and brilliant. Go nuts! But what Paul was doing was testing the waters.

Unlike the other women he'd dated who had upped and run when they sensed danger, Karla stayed. She absorbed all his kinks, easily submitted to his violent and degrading sexual desires, obeyed his every order, and accepted his constant criticism. Karla also went along with Paul controlling everything about her, from where she went, to what she ate, to what she thought, to how she dressed. She even started to write down all the ways in which she could improve herself for Paul.

Karla gave over total control and authority, and this is exactly what Paul wanted. Above all, Paul Bernardo was motivated by being able to dominate another person *completely*, while Karla was so submissive that she was driven by a need to be completely controlled. Do not, however, confuse her submissiveness with stupidity or fragility. Karla, as we'll see, was neither...

But none of this controlling behavior was obvious to others at first. Paul even moved in with the Homolkas and no one noticed anything odd *(even though Paul was such a giant asshole that he referred to the novel* American Psycho *as his bible, which is only slightly worse than when sales- people read* The Art of War *and talk about it at every opportunity, for the rest of their lives.)*

From the outside they seemed like the perfect pair. Karla loved that she had this older, sexy man because she felt that it gave her a boost in status.

And Paul loved that he had a younger, beautiful girlfriend who followed his every order. But soon it wasn't enough for him, and by December 1988 Paul had gone back to committing his violent rapes of strangers.

According to her later confessions, Karla knew what Paul was up to at this time, but it seems that she didn't really mind. For Paul, this would have set his "mur-dar" ringing—a term used by behavioral criminologist Gregg McCrary. What are we talking about? Let us explain: McCrary, who is a former FBI agent and actually worked on the Homolka/Bernardo case, said in a 2014 interview with *Psychology Today* that predators like Paul "often have a highly acute ability to detect potential co-conspirators, and just like there's radar [and] gaydar, maybe they have mur-dar."

We agree. Paul had sensed *something* in Karla; he saw her as someone who wouldn't be horrified by what he was. And he had been right, because now she was OK-ing the fact that he was a rapist. This was likely the first stage of Paul recognizing that, with his help, Karla could maybe go from a normal girl to an accomplice.

The Scarborough Rapist

Between 1987 and 1990, Paul Bernardo raped at least 19 women and girls in Scarborough, Ontario. These attacks usually involved a young victim being blitz-attacked in the street at night. He would threaten them with a knife and choke them with a garotte before raping them vaginally, anally, and orally. He would then force his victims to call themselves "sluts," give him their names, and all sorts of other personal information before he rubbed mud into their hair and threatened to kill them if they told the police.

The public was terrified and the police were stuck. None of the victims had been able to give a clear description of their attacker, until finally, on

May 26, 1990, one of the Scarborough Rapist's victims was able to work with police and create a composite sketch. The image was rapidly circulated around the Greater Toronto Area and it was a dead ringer for Paul Bernardo. In fact, the sketch looked so much like Paul that multiple people he knew came forward *independently* to report him, and Paul was interviewed by the police in November 1990. But in classic Bernardo fashion he didn't let this get him down. Paul spent the entire time joking around with the officers about how funny it was that he looked so similar to the composite sketch. He even willingly gave a sample of his DNA before walking out of the police station that day a free man.

Luckily for Paul, at the time DNA testing was still in its infancy, and on top of this, due to a series of clerical issues and oversights, his swab sat untested for *two whole years* alongside fifty thousand other samples. But Paul didn't know that this was the case. You'd think that after a brush with the law and his DNA now on record he might have laid low for a while, but that just wasn't Paul's style.

Tammy Homolka

Apart from all his constant criticisms about her appearance, her weight, and her intelligence, something else that Paul berated Karla about was her virginity, or lack thereof. As his "virgin farm" dream hints at, Paul was *obsessed* with female virginity. Karla's having lost hers before she and Paul had even met was to him akin to being unfaithful, and it was something he would never let her forget.

As this topic began to rear its head on a regular basis, Karla could feel Paul start to pull away. He was doing what he always did when she didn't give him what he wanted immediately. But this time—seeing as how she couldn't very well regain her virginity and give it to Paul on a silver platter—she was terrified that she would lose him for good. So it's theorized that Karla resolved to give him the next best thing: for his Christmas present that year, Karla decided to "gift" Paul her 15-year-old sister Tammy's virginity.

On the night of December 23, 1990, Karla and Paul spent a delightfully Christmassy evening with the Homolkas. After everyone else had stumbled up to bed *(pissed on eggnog or whatever other strange, festive cocktails North Americans seem to drink)*, the couple turned their sights on Tammy. They plied her with liquor laced with triazolam—a powerful tranquilizer that Karla had stolen from the veterinary clinic—and then they took the 15-year-old down to the basement.

Once Tammy was unconscious, Paul filmed Karla sexually assaulting her own sister. Then Karla used a rag soaked in halothane (a type of general anesthetic, that she had again stolen from the veterinary clinic) to keep Tammy unconscious while Paul proceeded to rape her. They filmed the entire ordeal, right up until the moment that Tammy choked on her own vomit and died.

Paul and Karla quickly put Tammy back in her bed and cleaned up the crime scene before calling 911. When they were questioned by police, they both claimed that Tammy had stayed up with them and just had too much to drink. Tammy's death was ruled accidental and no further questions were asked, even though she had a huge red burn on her face and lips. It was theorized that maybe it was just a burn from laying in her own vomit until the ambulance had arrived, but this burn had been caused by the halothane-soaked rag that Karla had used to keep Tammy knocked out.

After getting away with Tammy's murder, Karla and Paul's relationship was stronger than ever. They even stepped up their sex lives *(and by "stepped up," we mean took a major turn into perverse depravity)*, because they would sneak into Tammy's bedroom to reenact the crime over and over again. Karla would even wear her sister's clothes and dress up like a schoolgirl while Paul had sex with her on Tammy's bed.

We think this ability to "relive" the crime is a vital part of the motivation behind couples killing together. Serial killers tend to take trophies from their victims, which they do to relive the crime again and again. It reminds them of the kill, and much like any of us picking up a souvenir magnet while on vacation, it takes them back to a "happy" memory. We often see killers take jewelry so that they can have their unwitting wives, girlfriends, or children wear it. Every time the killer sees the trophy around the neck of a loved one, they are right back in the moment. With killer couples, however, they can become each other's trophies, and they now have a living, breathing reminder with whom they can relive the moment endlessly. The pair bonds over a secret that no one else knows. This could be a powerful motivator for a killer couple.

However, even *this* didn't hold Paul's attention for long and, although by now he and Karla were engaged, he started to sleep with other women. This isn't at all surprising; we think it's safe to say that Paul displays many of the signs of psychopathy, including being easily bored. And just like with solo serial killers, once the thrill of a kill wears off, they are right back to being dissatisfied, seeking excitement and more stimulation.

Desperate to up her game and get her man's attention back, on June 6, 1991, Karla invited a friend of hers—who we'll call Jane Doe—over to the house that she now shared with Paul. Once they were settled in, Karla handed Jane a drink spiked with the same tranquilizer she had used on Tammy, and then she called her fiancé to tell him to come home because she had a "wedding present" for him. That night, Paul and Karla sexually assaulted an unconscious Jane while filming the entire thing. When Jane finally woke up, she had absolutely no memory of the savagery she had just endured; she left the house sore and disoriented but alive.

After this disgusting "bonding experience," Paul was ready to commit to Karla. He cut all ties with the other women he had been sleeping with and just weeks later the couple got married. As you can see, Paul's response to Karla's participation in and enthusiasm for the rapes always delivered her desired results (e.g., he commits more). So it's possible that in her mind, no matter what lines she had to cross, her actions were always totally validated. This is because by this stage in the relationship, any moral compass that Karla ever had was completely broken. Keeping Paul interested and maintaining their relationship now had greater emotional significance to her than any qualms she may have had about the horrific things they were doing.

Leslie Mahaffy

On the very day Karla and Paul got married in their fairy-tale wedding—complete with horse and carriage—30 miles away in Burlington, a couple of canoers had come across eight blocks of cement with human body parts sticking out. The dismembered remains were determined to belong to a missing 14-year-old local girl named Leslie Mahaffy.

Karla had secured the couple's first two victims, but this time it had been Paul who had found and abducted Leslie. He had spotted her one night when she had been locked out of her house and he tricked her into his car with the promise of a cigarette. This speaks volumes as to Paul's charm and charisma; often male serial killers who lack confidence don't stand a chance of luring a female victim into their vehicles. This is actually often one of the key reasons that a male killer will pair up with a woman, because her presence usually puts potential victims at ease.

But Paul didn't *need* Karla to help him catch his prey; he could just turn on some of that classic Patrick Bateman charm. So it's clear that Karla served another purpose to him and his fantasy. What's also interesting to note is how different his MO was when he was working with Karla. When he operated solo, he blitz-attacked women in the street, but when he was with Karla he lured the victim back to their house. Although Paul was the dominant one, changing Karla, she was also influencing his behavior.

Once he had Leslie in the car, Paul drove straight home where he and Karla blindfolded her, raped her, and yet again videotaped the entire thing. Thanks to these tapes we know that 14-year-old Leslie's harrowing ordeal lasted for at least 24 hours. During this nightmare, her blindfold slipped off and she saw the faces of her attackers; tragically this probably sealed Leslie's fate. Karla gave Leslie a lethal dose of triazolam and then the young girl was strangled to death.

We can't know for sure if Leslie might have survived like Jane Doe had the blindfold not fallen off; we also can't definitively say exactly *who* did the strangling. Paul has always maintained that it was Karla who murdered Leslie, and she has always said it was him. It is interesting to note, however, that outside of his affiliation with Karla, Paul had never killed the women he had raped. *Even* when a woman he attacked had seen his face so clearly that she had been able to help police create that nearly perfect composite sketch. It wasn't until Paul started working with Karla that the murders began.

Could it be that this was Karla and Paul's MOs uniting? Like we mentioned, with killer couples there tends to be *a multiplying of motives* where both partners imprint their own motivations and desires on the crime. Paul, being a domineering sex offender, raped his victims, and Karla joined in to please him and to have that sick shared experience and connection. But could it be that it was *Karla* who wanted the girls killed afterward? Did she feel some sort of warped jealousy toward these victims who had been raped by her fiancé?

It's hard to say, but what lends credence to this theory is that even after the couple killed their first victim, Tammy, when Paul went back to attacking alone as the Scarborough Rapist, he didn't kill.

Kristen French

After the horrific discovery of Leslie Mahaffy, police didn't have long to take stock. The very next day, 15-year-old Kristen French's naked body was found in a ditch by the side of the road in northern Burlington. Kristen's battered body was covered in wounds consistent with brutal sexual and physical torture. Kristen had last been seen on April 16, 1992 in the parking lot of the Grace Lutheran Church in St. Catharines, Ontario; this is where Karla and Paul had spotted her. In a brazen move, they had grabbed Kristen and forced her into their car at knifepoint—all in broad daylight.

They took Kristen home and after three days of hell, Karla and Paul killed her. Again, just like with Leslie, it's not clear *who* actually did the strangulation, but the tapes would later clearly show a very enthusiastically participating Karla. By this point in their killing careers, Karla and Paul were also trying to take forensic countermeasures more seriously; they had thoroughly washed Kristen's body and even shaved off all her hair. But despite their best attempts, DNA *was* recovered by investigators and it was a match to the Scarborough Rapist. Now the police knew they were looking for one man in connection to all these crimes.

Breakups

Eventually, Ken and Barbie's murderous relationship came to a violent end. Paul had always been abusive toward Karla, but in January 1993 he beat her so badly that her eye partially dislodged from its socket, and she ended up in the emergency room. Karla's family had had enough; they begged her to leave Paul. She finally agreed. Karla even reluctantly gave in to their demands that she report Paul for what he'd done.

This trip by Karla to the police station is an *interesting* one to say the least. She turned up with two black eyes and told authorities about her abusive husband; *that* was all pretty horrifically ordinary. But she was wearing something that stood out. Officers noticed she wore a very distinctive Mickey Mouse watch that looked exactly like the one that 15-year-old Kristen French had been wearing when she disappeared.

A couple of weeks after this domestic abuse report—*finally*, after two years—Paul Bernardo's DNA was matched to the Scarborough Rapist's. The police and the Green Ribbon Task Force (set up to investigate the murders of Leslie and Kristen) connected the dots and realized that not only was Paul Bernardo their man, but also that his wife had already been in to see them.

On February 9, Toronto Metro police arrived at Karla's house to question her. They told her that Paul was a suspect in a series of rapes; at first she played dumb and acted shocked, but Karla's tone changed when they asked her about the Mickey Mouse watch. Karla, now realizing that this was serious, kept her mouth shut. When the police finally left—after five hours of questioning her—Karla confessed to her family that Paul was indeed the Scarborough Rapist and that she needed a lawyer ASAP.

Karla told her lawyer everything, and she made it clear that she was willing to cooperate in exchange for a plea bargain. The prosecutors were desperate for Karla's testimony against Paul; sure, they had the DNA match, but if Karla took the stand their case would be rock solid. It seems odd for our modern crime brains to take this in—if anything, juries these days *only* want to see DNA evidence. But in the early nineties, DNA testing wasn't something that was in the public consciousness like it is today. After all, DNA had only become admissible in court approximately four years prior, in 1988.

The police saw Karla as their ace in the hole. She was the perfect witness— a young, pretty woman—and *herself* a victim of the killer's abuse. Karla also promised the detectives even *more* evidence against Paul. She told them that if they searched the couple's house they would find dozens of hidden videotapes detailing all the rapes and murders. Karla also said that these tapes would show that she had just been an innocent bystander—a passive and battered woman forced to take part by her abusive husband and too terrified to stop him.

The Tapes

On February 17, 1993, Paul Bernardo was arrested at his home for the murders of Leslie Mahaffy and Kristen French and for the crimes of the Scarborough Rapist. With Bernardo in cuffs, a 71-day search of his house began. But police didn't find the stacks of incriminating videotapes that Karla Homolka had promised. They only found one that showed Karla performing oral sex on an unidentified girl. Karla stuck to her story that Paul had forced her to do it. It would be years before that girl would be proven to be her own sister, Tammy Homolka.

And so a deal was struck. Karla was allowed to plead guilty to just two counts of manslaughter on the condition that she testify against her estranged husband in court. Karla's trial kicked off on June 28, 1993, and two weeks later on July 6 she was convicted and sentenced to serve two concurrent 12-year prison sentences. Unbeknownst to police and prosecutors, their initial search of Bernardo's home had missed several videotapes that would have shown the true extent of Karla Homolka's involvement.

Worse still, these tapes were recovered by Bernardo's lawyer on May 6, 1993—*before* Karla's trial. This lawyer, however, decided to keep them to himself, planning to surprise Karla on the stand. These tapes—which showed in stomach-churningly graphic detail the torture of Tammy Homolka, Leslie Mahaffy, Jane Doe, and Kristen French—were not turned over to police until September 22, 1994!

Watching them, it was clear to police and prosecutors that Karla was no innocent bystander. In some of the videos she can even be seen and heard directing the shots. It was a stark and disturbing realization for investigators, but it had come far too late. Karla had already been tried, and due to double jeopardy laws, she was never charged with any of the crimes caught on tape. This earned her plea deal the title "deal with the devil."

Had these tapes been discovered *before* Karla's trial, her testimony wouldn't have been needed, and it's almost certain that she would have been sentenced to more than 12 years. Karla could easily have been shown to be lying and misleading police during the investigation. For example, she lied about things like Jane Doe and Paul having been close, when in fact Jane Doe was *her* friend, and it was very provable that Paul didn't know her.

This lie may not seem like a big deal, but there were many inconsistencies in Karla's stories. When she took the stand at Paul's trial, any holes that the defense poked in her story, Karla would just say that the abuse had been so bad it had destroyed her memory. But there were *no* consequences for Karla's lying; the prosecutors had made their bed thanks to the deal they'd cut and now they just wanted to remain fully focused on nailing Paul.

By the time Paul Bernardo's trial kicked off on May 1, 1995, all the videotapes had of course been found so there was no point in him denying the rapes and torture. But Paul did deny that he had killed Leslie or Kristen—he put that squarely on Karla. When Karla was cross-examined by the defense, they posed the theory that she hadn't been *forced* to do anything, and that she had in fact loved every second of the couple's torture sessions. The defense even pointed to evidence that suggested that Kristen and Leslie hadn't been killed by strangulation, but that Leslie had been smothered to death and Kristen had died of a head trauma. Both acts, the defense argued, were carried out by Karla. Throughout this questioning Karla stayed calm, and simply kept saying either that she couldn't remember or that it was all Paul.

The jury deliberated for just one day before finding Paul Bernardo guilty on all counts and he was sentenced to life in prison without the possibility of parole. Karla Homolka was released in 2005, at which point she quickly moved to Quebec to start over again. She got remarried, had three children, and has seemingly led a normal life. Karla has even been able to volunteer at an elementary school in Montreal(!), because she was never placed on a sex offender registry. To this day, Karla Homolka has never been charged with a single sex crime despite there being video proof of her involvement in the rape and murder of at least four girls.

Personality

We've talked a lot about our thoughts on Karla and Paul's motivations in this chapter, but let's now discuss what personality or mental disorders *might* have been at play. This is really important in helping us to understand Karla's culpability and agency in this entire situation.

From the start, police almost immediately assumed that Karla was a "compliant victim," despite there being signs indicating the opposite. Now, we're not ignoring the fact that she was a victim of Paul—he did abuse her—but as we detail in the sidebar to the right, there are *big* differences between Karla and the typical compliant victim. Most of the compliant victim women studied were poorly educated, socially isolated, and lacking in any kind of confidence, and they had also all invariably suffered physical or sexual abuse from a young age.

These factors just do not fit Karla's background, and it wasn't until all the other horrendous tapes showing her excitedly and enthusiastically engaging in the rapes and torture were discovered did police realize just how involved she'd been.

COMPLIANT VICTIMS OF SEXUAL SADISTS

During their investigation into the murders of Leslie Mahaffy and Kristen French, the Royal Canadian Mounted Police (RCMP) met with the FBI to discuss potential criminal profiles of their killer. During this process, the RCMP were presented with the 1993 paper "Compliant Victims of the Sexual Sadist," written by Robert Hazelwood, a former FBI special agent, and Janet Warren, a professor of clinical psychiatric medicine.

The study surveyed seven women serving serious prison time as a result of helping their spouses commit violent offenses. It described a compliant victim as "the romantic partner of a sexual sadist who, due to psychological conditioning, aided the sexual sadist in activities that were against their own interests, such as criminal acts or enduring pain." It concluded that these women's criminal activities had been resulted from the brutal treatment they had suffered at the hands of their partners.

These women were also usually just spectators in the crimes rather than active participants. When their backgrounds were examined, it was found that all of these women had low self-esteem, dependent personality disorders, a poor education, extreme social isolation, and a long history of physical and sexual abuse.

When this paper came out in 1993, the concept that a woman could be transformed into a dependent accomplice through abuse was fairly new, but it became very en vogue in law enforcement circles. So, when a trail of clues led the RCMP to Karla Homolka's doorstep, the investigators were already primed to see her as a woman beaten into submission by Paul Bernardo, a domineering sexual sadist.

You could argue that Karla just went along with the attacks because it was what Paul wanted, but it doesn't mean that she didn't enjoy it. She was still getting something out of it. All too often criminal analysis assumes that women lack any agency, but Karla was separated from Paul when she went to the police station to report him, wearing the watch of a girl they had tortured and murdered. That was a choice she made and a trophy she kept. That doesn't sound like a passive, terrified accomplice, does it?

After she was jailed, a mental health professional diagnosed Karla with post-traumatic stress disorder and battered woman syndrome. But there is still, in our opinion, a lot of room for doubt and there are plenty of experts who agree. Many say that right from the start Karla's antisocial tendencies were totally ignored or at least minimized. As referenced in the book *Homicide: A Forensic Psychology Casebook,* psychiatry professor Dr. Graham Glancy believes that the most likely scenario is that Karla had histrionic personality disorder combined with a condition called *hybristophilia*—a theory that has been backed up by the reanalysis of Karla's scores from the Minnesota Multiphasic Personality Inventory (the most popular clinical assessment tool used to help diagnose mental health disorders).

Hybristophilia: Bad Boys for Life

According to professor of forensic psychology Dr. Katherine Ramsland, hybristophilia is a "sexual disorder in which arousal is contingent on being with a partner who has committed an outrage, such as rape, torture, or murder." It is a sexual disorder that can be separated into two categories: passive and active.

Passive hybristophiliacs have no interest in actually participating in the object of their affection's crimes. These are the ones who send family annihilator Chris Watts banana bread in prison because they think he's cute and misunderstood. Even the Night Stalker, Richard Ramirez, found love with Doreen Lioy while he was in prison.

Karla Homolka, on the other hand, is, in our opinion, most definitely the poster girl for *active* hybristophilia. For her, it seems that there was a thrill in knowing that she was with such a dangerous man and the tapes suggest she enjoyed actively participating in his crimes. We don't think that Karla Homolka was tricked by Paul Bernardo—she was most definitely drawn to him for what a shitbag he was *(even if "shitbag" may not feature in the official definition of hybristophilia)*.

So, why are some women turned on by killers and dangerous men? There are many theories, including the idea that these women just get a rush from being close to someone who others are terrified of. It can give the woman a weird ego boost to know that her partner is dangerous, even a cold-blooded killer, but that he loves *her*. She can tell herself that it must be because she is special in some way. It can also be a weird sort of defense mechanism—if you're already with the most dangerous man out there, who else could hurt you? As far as those women like Doreen Lioy are concerned, they may romanticize things and believe that they can change the murderous man they love so much. In some cases, they may even be convinced that he is actually innocent. Or, at the very least it's a self-preservation tactic—after all, in prison he can't abandon them, hurt them, or be unfaithful.

Finally, studies like the 2018 paper "Do Psychopathic Birds of a Feather Flock Together?" show that women with extreme personalities tend to be drawn to men with extreme personalities. If Karla does have antisocial personality disorder or histrionic personality disorder, either condition would indicate her being highly prone to seeking stimulation. And when two extreme individuals come together, the attachment behavior and the way in which they connect is usually incredibly intense, dependent, and aggressive. It creates a union that, given the right conditions in each partner, could be like a nuclear bomb going off.

So, let's wrap this chapter up with our final thoughts on Karla and Paul. We think it's safe to say that even if Paul had never met Karla—or someone like her—Paul would have still continued to rape women. He probably would have escalated, and it's likely that eventually he would have killed. But with Karla—while she would likely have been a callous and intense person—we think it's unlikely she would have ever been involved in such a series of crimes on her own.

When it comes to deadly duos, whether the submissive partner is a passive or active participant in the crimes, there are very few who are *totally* innocent. And killer couples like Karla Homolka and Paul Bernardo—just like normal romantic couples—each get something that they need from the other. Paul needed Karla's total loyalty in order to validate himself, and Karla wanted Paul's dominance, authority, and love. For this, she was willing to pay any price. Maybe being single isn't so bad, regardless of what our mothers think.

BIGOTRY

The Less-Dead, Lingerie, and Looking the Other Way

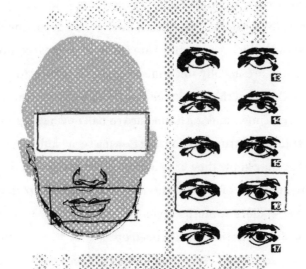

THIS IS GOING TO BE A BIT OF A MYTH-BUSTING CHAPTER, so let's kick off with a myth we see thrown around constantly—that serial killers *want* to get caught.

Serial killers escalate with each kill, either stepping up the brutality of their methods or the risks of their hunt. But this isn't because they *want* to get caught. Rather, it's usually because they develop a feeling of invincibility and start to think that they *can't* get caught. This is when they start making mistakes. As Ted Bundy put it, "You learn what you need to kill and take care of the details. It's like changing a tire. The first time you're careful. By the thirtieth time, you can't remember where you left the lug wrench."

It's usually when a serial killer starts to get sloppy that they get caught, because generally speaking, regardless of the police department leading the charge, serial killer investigations are some of the most complex cases to crack. Victims are usually unconnected, i.e., unknown to each other and the killer. On top of this, the killer may be transient and move around to commit their crimes, making them hard to nail down geographically.

Even if police are struggling to track down a serial killer, you would at least hope that they know they have a multiple murderer on their hands. But there are instances of serial killers who, for years, completely slipped through the net—killers no one had even been looking for. And victims who went unnoticed, even as their bodies piled up.

Who are these killers? Well, for starters, chances are their victims are the "less-dead."

The idea of the less-dead—typically people from racial minorities; members of the LGBTQ community; sex workers; the homeless; people with mental health challenges; people with learning disabilities; or people with substance abuse issues—is nothing new to most true crime enthusiasts. The sad fact is that individuals, society, and our institutions subconsciously rank the value of a person's life based on a few key factors and there is a bias that some victims are more worthy than others. This empathy gap that exists for the less-dead can reveal itself in some pretty unsavory ways, from massively varying levels of media attention to the manner in which police investigate certain crimes. In this chapter, we're going to take a look at how institutional and societal bigotry leads to the continued marginalization and discrimination of certain individuals and communities.

Let's put our stat hats on for a minute to take this all in. Recently, the *Washington Post* mapped out more than 52,000 murders spanning the last 10 years, covering 52 of the United States' largest cities. Shockingly, they found that half of these homicides (26,000) saw no arrest being made by police, and that in 18,600 of those 26,000 murders—so in almost three-quarters of the cases—the victim had been Black.

Digging deeper into the figures, the *Washington Post* also discovered that while police arrested someone in 63 percent of cases where the murder victim was white, arrests were only made 47 percent of the time when the victim was Black. Although Black victims make up the majority of homicides in most cities (Black Americans account for 68 percent of all homicide victims in the 52 largest cities in the US), they were the least likely of any racial group to have their killings result in an arrest. In almost every city the *Washington Post* examined, arrests were made in the killings of Black victims at lower rates than homicides involving white victims; the gap was largest in Boston, where in 2007, of the 435 homicides with Black victims, 254 remained unsolved, but of the 57 homicides with white victims only six were still unsolved.

If that sounds bad, it's only about to get a whole lot worse, because while recent events and the rise of the BLM movement have shone an unignorable light on the unacceptable policing of Black communities—particularly

Black men—there is also an absolute epidemic of violence bubbling up against Black trans women in the US.

According to the Human Rights Campaign, 110 trans women were killed in the US between 2014 and 2019, and 88 of these victims were Black and 11 were Latinx. That means a staggering 90 percent of *all* trans women killed during that period were Black or Latinx. When you pick apart more statistics, you'll see that UCLA School of Law's Williams Institute found that around 55 percent of all transgender adults are white, and only 16 percent and 21 percent identify as Black and Latinx, respectively. It is undeniable that Black and Latinx trans women are being killed at a rate hugely disproportionate to their white counterparts.

Then, just to rub salt in an already painful wound, only 42 percent of these murders of Black trans women resulted in an arrest. When you compare this to FBI stats that suggest around 61 percent of murders among the general population result in an arrest, it's hard to pretend there isn't an issue. Numbers, unlike police, don't lie.

There are obviously myriad reasons why these sad statistics are the case; racism and bigotry being two big gross things that jump to mind immediately. But these issues are dismissed by some as being hard to substantiate. However, let's stick it to the deniers and consider what ProPublica found in 2018—that of the 85 transgender murders that occurred during that time, police referred to 74 of the victims by names and genders they no longer used. So in almost 90 percent of cases that year, police were running around asking questions about murder victims and getting their entire identities wrong. Is it any surprise then that arrests often are not made?

But there are other factors *(besides the police using the wrong names, genders, and descriptions of the victims)* that may feed into why there are such a high percentage of unsolved, uninvestigated murders within these demographics. Black people and communities of color in the US, along with members of the LGBTQ+ community, may be less willing to engage with the police due to previous negative experiences with them, such as police brutality and harassment. If people are less keen to chat with the police, it will obviously make solving the crimes harder—but this isn't us letting the police off the hook. It should be the police's responsibility to repair damage done and trust destroyed between their institution and the public.

Trust has not only been eroded with these groups, but also with sex workers. The profession is as old as time and has been discriminated against for just as long. We'd be hard pressed to find a group less trusting of the police, not to mention the media. Even when the press decides to cover or acknowledge the murders of sex workers, the reporting often undermines these victims and emphasizes and compounds society's apathy toward them.

For example, after the 2013 murder of Tracy Connelly in Melbourne, Australia, many local newspapers featured the phrase "prostitute murdered" in their headlines. This term *prostitute* is synonymous in our society with something "dirty" or "sinful," and by labeling Connelly that way, the papers—intentionally or not—distanced her from being an empathic victim. The media even noted that Connelly must have been aware of the dangers of her profession; this sort of reporting shifts the blame to the victim by implying that they got themselves into that mess and that it was their choice—that somehow, they deserved what happened to them. It also gives the reader an out for any lack of empathy or secret judgment they may be feeling.

As we've seen, there are some huge disparities in how different groups and demographics are policed, and in the way in which some are discussed in the media when they become victims of violent crimes. But how has this shaped the way we think? After a bit of head-scratching, we've identified two big myths when it comes to our collective thinking around serial killers and their victims. These myths, in our humble opinion, have mainly been perpetrated by the media and Hollywood in a joint marketing venture to make more cash money off serial killer movies and true crime stories. So it's time we did some serious myth-busting.

MYTH 1: *The majority of serial killer victims are beautiful, young white women who only wear negligees to bed.*

This is of course false—no points for having guessed that; we literally labeled it "Myth 1." But firstly, no one wears a negligee to bed; many have tried, all have morphed into Sweatzilla and given up. These days women wear their favorite true crime podcast's merch covered in dog/cat hair to bed. That's not very sellable, though. But despite what the movies want us to believe, the truth is that the majority of serial killer victims are among the less-dead.

Why is this the case? Well, of course there is a low-hanging fruit element to this; some of these victims, such as sex workers, do lead higher-risk lifestyles. But like we discovered through the stats we shared earlier, far too often deeply entrenched institutional bigotry tragically stands in the way of justice for many. And this kind of bigotry—be it racist, homophobic, transphobic, or misogynistic—within law enforcement and the media has serious ramifications. It can lead to certain cases being overlooked. Consider for a moment the case of Stephen Port (a.k.a. the Grindr Killer, a.k.a. the Cemetery Poisoner) and London's most recent serial killer.

In 2014, Stephen Port was a 41-year-old chef living alone in Barking, East London. (He even made a surprise background appearance in that year's UK *MasterChef*, spotted behind that guy from boy band JLS making meatballs . . .) As Port's first moniker suggests, he used hookup app Grindr to find and lure young gay men to his flat. Port would then give these unsuspecting men fatal doses of the drug GHB (gamma-hydroxybutyric acid), better known as the date rape drug. He would then rape his victims and make their deaths look like accidental overdoses or suicides.

Port had a fetish for having sex with unconscious boyish-looking young men he called twinks. All four of Port's victims (Anthony Walgate, 23; Gabriel Kovari, 22; Daniel Whitworth, 21; and Jack Taylor, 25) were young, boyish, similar-looking gay men in their twenties and they all died of GHB overdoses within 15 months of each other. Their bodies were found just meters apart; in fact, Whitworth and Kovari were found in the *exact same spot* by the exact same terrified dog walker.

Despite overwhelming evidence to the contrary and uproar from the men's friends and family, for over a year the police maintained their stance that these four men had simply died from partying too hard at one of London's gay nightclubs. It's unbelievable that the London Metropolitan Police (not some tiny police force in the middle of nowhere with no clue how to run a homicide investigation) totally missed the fact that they had a serial killer on their hands.

Port is now serving a whole-of-life sentence, convicted of 22 offenses against 11 men, including four murders, four rapes, four assaults by penetration, and 10 offenses of administering a substance with intent. It was thanks to the work of Kovari's good friend John Pape and Taylor's sisters that this case was eventually cracked. *(They had to shout extremely loudly to be heard over the institutional homophobia.)* It's hard to imagine that if four white middle-class women had turned up dead, just roads apart, two in the same cemetery, that the police wouldn't have taken it all a bit more seriously.

Port was not a calculated killer; actually, he was a very careless one. Just look at his lazy body disposals—and that's our point. Despite his stupidity, Port was able to kill four men and slip under the radar of the London Metropolitan Police because he went after gay men. The police discriminated against these victims by dismissing them as drug addicts. This sort of thinking by law enforcement gives serial killers more calculated and cunning than Port the green light to go after the less-dead. Because they know that if they do, they might be able to go on killing for a much longer period of time. Sadly, this dark hypothesis bears out. You will often see that the serial killers who racked up the highest body counts tended to target marginalized victims; consider Jeffrey Dahmer and Gary Heidnik.

Gary Heidnik was actually one of the men who, along with lampshade lad Ed Gein, inspired the character of Buffalo Bill in *The Silence of the Lambs*. Old Ed gave Bill his skin-wearing aesthetic, but Heidnik was very much the menacing real-life architect for the pit in which Bill's victims had to "put the lotion on the skin."

Heidnik was an egomaniac who needed to be admired, so he started a church in his own house at 3520 North Marshall Street, Philadelphia. He used this organization to line his pockets, lure vulnerable young women, and provide himself with a cover of respectability. During this time, Heidnik claimed that God spoke to him and demanded that he father as many children as possible, but Heidnik had failed to hold down marriages due to his wives not enjoying being his punching bag on the daily. Heidnik knew if he abducted women from the church, he'd get caught, so he did the next most obvious thing—he built a pit in his basement and started to abduct Black women, some of them sex workers.

Eventually, Heidnik had six women chained up and sealed into his basement pit: Josefina Rivera, 25; Sandra Lindsay, 24; Lisa Thomas, 19; Deborah Dudley, 23; Jacqueline Askins, 18; and Agnes Adams, 24. Heidnik believed that these women were inferior to him and everyone else. He also knew that the police probably wouldn't be looking very hard into what had happened to missing members of the less-dead.

As described by Ken Englade in his book, *Cellar of Horror*, the tortures Heidnik doled out are some of the worst in the world of true crime: he raped, beat, and electrocuted the women. Some days he would go down to the basement, wrap duct tape around the heads of his victims, and then drive screwdrivers into their ears. When the women would rebel against him he would fill the pit with water and deliver jolts of agonizing electricity. When Heidnik killed Sandra Lindsay, just to add to the psychological torment for the other women, Heidnik dragged Deborah Dudley upstairs to show them Lindsay's remains. Lindsay's head was in a pot, her ribs were in a roasting pan on the stove, and her legs and arms were in the freezer. After this, he starved the women for weeks and then fed them a nightmarish gruel of dog food mixed with Sandra Lindsay's remains.

Over the four months he kept these women captive, Heidnik started to become overconfident. No one suspected him, his plan was working, and he was having a great time. In his mind, these stupid women were like animals and he was the master; he had total control. But it was this arrogance that blinded him and Josefina Rivera was about to take the upper hand.

In March 1987, Heidnik announced that he was going on the hunt for another victim, to which Josefina Rivera (who had slowly been manipulating Heidnik into thinking she was his brainwashed slave) offered to help. Rivera helped Heidnik abduct Agnes Adams that day, but she had no intention of Adams suffering for long. Rivera managed to convince Heidnik to let her go for just a few minutes so that she could see her family. Rivera told him to wait at a petrol station and that she wouldn't be long; she just wanted to tell her family that she was OK.

Heidnik agreed. Josefina Rivera calmly walked around the corner to where she knew Heidnik wouldn't be able to see her, and then ran to the nearest pay phone and called 911. Within minutes, the police had arrived and Heidnik was arrested right there and then. Rivera then led the police to 3520 North Marshall Street and finally, the women were freed. Two women lost their lives at the hands of Gary Heidnik and if Josefina Rivera hadn't done what she did, it's hard to say how many more women he would have abducted, tortured, and killed—because as we know, he was most certainly the type of killer who wouldn't have stopped until he was caught.

Much more famous serial killer Jeffrey Dahmer (a.k.a. the Milwaukee Cannibal, a.k.a. the Milwaukee Monster), like Heidnik, knew exactly how to keep his crimes under wraps. Dahmer chose to live in an incredibly impoverished part of Milwaukee; he suspected that there police officers would be unlikely to take much notice of what he was up to, and he was right. Dahmer also knew to go after marginalized men. He predominately sought out Black, Asian, and Latin men; in fact 11 of Dahmer's 17 known victims were Black.

We'll never really know how many men Dahmer killed (given that he was beaten to death by another prisoner in 1994), but he killed *at least* 17 men and boys between 1987 and 1991: Steven Hicks, 18; Steven Tuomi, 26; Jamie Doxtator, 14; Richard Guerrero, 25; Anthony Sears, 24; Eddie Smith, 36; Ricky Beeks, 27; Ernest Miller, 22; David Thomas, 23; Curtis Straughter, 16; Errol Lindsey, 19; Tony Hughes, 31; Konerak Sinthasomphone, 14; Matt Turner, 20; Jeremiah Weinberger, 23; Oliver Lacy, 23; and Joseph Bradeholt, 25. (There is contradictory information out there on the men's ages and some of these are approximations.)

While Dahmer was killing all these men, he wasn't living in a remote Wisconsin farmhouse in the middle of nowhere—he lived in an apartment in the city surrounded by neighbors. How this went uninvestigated *should* be totally baffling, especially considering Dahmer would keep the remains of his victims on the property and even use a chainsaw to dismember the bodies. But really, we know why—the people raising the alarm were all poor and Black.

Race relations in the city had been in a state of total disarray for nearly a decade by the time Dahmer was boiling bodies, so it's safe to say the police were less involved because victims were Black and people of color. On top of this, the Milwaukee police at the time couldn't have been less keen to investigate what they deemed "gay" issues. At trial Dahmer maintained that his victim selection was not racist but based on his sexual preference, but we, like his victims' families, don't believe it. He knew that the race of these victims would make it easier for him to carry on doing what he was doing.

So what was he doing? Well, Jeffrey Dahmer would lure men and boys back to his apartment where he would drug them, and once they were incapacitated Dahmer would experiment. As Jack Rosewood outlines in his 2017 book, *Jeffrey Dahmer: A Terrifying Story of Rape, Murder, and Cannibalism*, at first Dahmer killed his victims straight away by cutting their throats, then he'd pose them for photos and try to preserve their bodies or body parts. Dahmer wanted to possess his victims. He didn't want them to leave him, but he also didn't want a real-life human to be around because they were altogether too much trouble.

When he was eventually asked about the various preservation techniques he used, Dahmer said, "I wanted to keep them, but if I couldn't keep them there with me whole, I at least could keep their skeletons." But soon he realized that these grisly human trinkets (including the decapitated frozen heads of his victims and pickled penises) weren't enough to satisfy his sick sexual urges. He realized that he wanted, above all else, a sex zombie.

On April 7, 1991, Dahmer lured 19-year-old Errol Lindsey to his apartment. He drugged him, drilled a hole in Lindsey's skull, and then poured hydrochloric acid into it. Dahmer was hoping that this would enable Lindsey to stay alive but keep him in a subdued and permanently submissive sex zombie state. According to Dahmer's later police interviews, Lindsey woke up after the acid was in and said, "I have a headache. What time is it?" Sad that his experiment had failed, Dahmer strangled Errol Lindsey to death.

Undeterred, he tried again. On the afternoon of May 26, 1991, Dahmer met a 14-year-old Laotian boy named Konerak Sinthasomphone. He offered him some money to go back to his place for a photo shoot, and the kid agreed. Once home, Dahmer drugged the teenager, drilled a hole into his skull, and then just like with Errol Lindsey, he poured acid into his head. He then led the boy into his bedroom where the decaying corpse of another man, Tony Hughes, lay. He put Konerak to bed and lay with him for a while and knocked back a few beers. And then—perhaps having run out of booze—Dahmer decided to pop out to a bar.

While Dahmer was out, at around 2 a.m., unbelievably the 14-year-old regained consciousness and managed to get out of Dahmer's apartment. He was clearly heavily drugged, he was naked, and he was bleeding from the hole in his head. Konerak was found by two young Black women, Nichole Childress and Sandra Smith, who called the police, but then Dahmer, who was coming home from his trip to the bar, saw what was going on. He tried to grab Konerak and drag him back inside, but the women stopped him; they knew something was terribly wrong.

When four officers arrived, Dahmer just told them that Konerak was his boyfriend and that he was just a bit drunk and he needed to get him back inside. The women were outraged; they demanded that the police help the clearly injured boy, but the police believed white adult Dahmer and even threatened to arrest the women if they didn't stop. The police actually *helped* Dahmer get Konerak back into his apartment—an apartment with another human body in the bedroom and various dismembered extremities filling up the fridge!

Dahmer was arrested two months later when another man escaped from his apartment and called the police. After this, the families of Dahmer's victims filed a lawsuit against the officers who had handed 14-year-old Konerak Sinthasomphone back to Dahmer on May 27, 1991. It turned out that the police hadn't even done a basic background check on Dahmer. If they had, they would have discovered that he was actually on probation at the time for having sexually assaulted another minor in 1988, and that minor was none other than Konerak's own brother!

Despite police denials that race and sexuality had anything to do with their lack of curiosity over what Dahmer had been up to, we have receipts. The recordings of calls made by the responding officers immediately after they left the scene in which they can be heard laughing at Konerak and saying that they needed "delousing" tell a somewhat different story.

The families' lawsuit alleged the Milwaukee police department had "a longstanding practice of intentional discrimination against and reckless disregard of the rights of racial minorities and homosexuals." We find it impossible to believe that had the situation been reversed and the police had found an older Black man trying to wrestle a 14-year-old white boy—who was drugged out of his mind and bleeding from his head while two white women screamed in the street that the boy needed help—that the police would have led the little boy into the apartment of his killer.

It would appear that the city wasn't all that confident with their case either, seeing as how they settled the lawsuit out of court and paid $850,000 to Konerak Sinthasomphone's family. Two of the officers involved in the incident on May 27 were eventually fired following the lawsuit. They were still given a full pension.

Even the notorious Albert Fish—the horrific "Grey Man"—preyed predominantly on Black children for years, but his downfall only came about when he killed Grace Budd, a 10-year-old white girl.

Now, both Heidnik and Dahmer were white men targeting victims of color. But usually, serial killers tend to kill within their own race, so the irony of us ignoring victims of color has led to the bizarre, but highly popular misconception, that there's no such thing as a non-white serial killer. Well, it's time for equal opportunity horror, guys, and this leads us nicely into our next myth. *Queens of the seggie strike again.*

MYTH 2: *Only white men are serial killers.*

We've all seen the memes saying that dressing up like a serial killer on Halloween if you aren't white is white cultural appropriation, and sure, we've laughed at them too because they're funny. But—and sorry to be that "well, actually" wanker—pop culture's obsession with the idea that only white men are serial killers is *dangerous.*

In this chapter alone we have already named three white male serial killers that nine out of ten of you probably already knew about. Bundy, Dahmer, and Heidnik are all household names, but the truth is that serial killers are usually as diverse as the country in which they kill. White men do not monopolize serial killing in the West; it's just historically been white male killers like Bundy who have transcended into uncomfortable, unlikely, glamorous pop culture icons—and the media are all too happy to help them out.

How deeply rooted is this idea? Well, let's do a quick test. If we asked you to reel off the names of serial killers you know, how long would it be before you got to a Black or non-white serial killer? Our money says quite a while.

Caroline Picart and John Browning explore this idea in their book *Speaking of Monsters*. They posit that the popular misconception that all serial killing is done by white males is due to the continuous cinematic depiction of just that. After all, how many Hollywood movies can you think of that focus on a non-white serial killer? *Switchback* is all we've got.

Indeed, serial killers span all racial groups; there is nothing unique about it to white men. Think about it: serial killers are active in every nation in the world, and while yes, the US does by quite a considerable measure top the charts, serial killers in a country like America are as racially diverse as the population itself. In fact, studies have shown that there is an *overrepresentation* of Black serial killers in the US.

In his 2005 paper "African-Americans and Serial Killing in the Media: The Myth and the Reality," Anthony Walsh, an American criminologist and professor at Boise State University, examined 58 years of serial killing activity in the US between 1945 and 2004. In this study, Walsh found there to be 90 African American serial killers and 323 white American serial killers active within the timeframe of the study. When you compare these numbers by proportion within the population, African Americans were represented among serial killers at a rate approximately *twice* their average percentage in the population (which was about 10.5 percent) across the same timeframe.

Black serial killers are most certainly a thing; in fact, they disproportionately "outperform" their white counterparts in terms of their sheer numbers. (And given that studies like this are only considering *known* serial killers, this can only be the tip of the iceberg.) So, if the existing data shows this—and reports point it out—why then is the reality of the Black serial killer not talked about?

Why is it that these men don't achieve the celebrity status of a Bundy and make it into those weird Etsy serial killer coloring books? Why aren't they being played by a former *High School Musical* cast member in a turtleneck? Why do society and the media fall all over themselves to paint serial killers as exclusively white men? Why do we ignore Black and other minority serial killers?

The most obvious reason that jumps to mind is, of course, that since serial killers usually kill within their own race, most serial killers of color kill victims of color. Victims of color are the less-dead and therefore we don't hear about them. But given that Heidnik and Dahmer, who both targeted victims of color, are well-known serial killers, this can't be the whole story . . .

One theory out there is that media outlets limit coverage of Black serial killers and other serial killers of color because of a fear they will be accused of racism. In his paper, Walsh makes this particular claim. He suggests that the media is too scared to "cover heinous crimes committed by African Americans compared with the zealousness of its coverage of such crimes committed by whites."

This is an interesting theory, but not one we can get on board with. Why? Well, let's consider the media's willingness and the ease with which they cover stories featuring minorities as petty criminals, gangbangers, or drug dealers. What about terrorism? Is it only terrorism if the assailant is a brown Muslim man with a beard? Because according to most Western media white nationalist terrorism isn't really terrorism, and an angry white man who goes on a politically motivated rampage is often seen as a "lone wolf."

Interestingly, white men *do* lead the pack when it comes to crimes like shootings, domestic terrorism, and family annihilations, and although they are consistently the most likely profile of such killers, this isn't the narrative the media seems to present. Yet in the world of serial killing, where statistically white men *aren't* that unique, we're constantly being force fed their weird serial killing big dick energy and it's fascinating. We theorize that possibly this is because being a terrorist or killing your family isn't deemed quite as "romantic" as being a serial killer. Perhaps a terrorist isn't quite as "fuckable" as a serial killer.

Think about those women who used to dress up like the 30 women Bundy raped and murdered down to the dyed, middle-parted brown hair and hoop earrings to go be his groupies at trial. And look at how people today *still* look at that creepy-faced weirdo and tell you he's hot. Even Dahmer got a mess of love letters from a load of female fans, even though he definitely wasn't buying what they were selling.

Leave alone for a minute the wackos turning up at trial in victim fancy-dress, sending in these letters and gifts and marrying locked up serial murderers. Society itself has fallen in love with serial killers; they totally dominate popular culture and entertainment today. *(Look no further than us, your friendly neighborhood true crime podcasters . . .)* Serial killers are fetishized by society as being geniuses. They outsmart everyone; they are always 10 steps ahead; they're omnipotent, dominant, powerful. Sexy, right? Do we ignore serial killers of color because society and the media are happy to readily apply these traits to white men but not to men of color?

So now we can start to understand why the prevalent myth that serial killers are rarely Black has two detrimental effects: First, it seems to suggest that African Americans are not sufficiently psychologically complex or intelligent to commit a series of murders without being caught. Second, police tend to neglect the protection of potential victims of serial killers in African American communities.

In fact, any race-based assumptions made by law enforcement when it comes to the criminality of a certain demographic have a terrible impact on the whole of society. Now, some will say that this is all nonsense and that it's not about racism at all. These people tend to claim that Bundy, Dahmer, Gacy, et al. just got more coverage because they had so many victims and because their crimes were so brutal.

Again, we have to call bullshit on this. Just consider for a moment that the FBI have now confirmed that Samuel Little, a Black drifter killer who was caught in 2012, is now America's most prolific serial killer *ever*. He is thought to have killed upwards of 90 people between 1970 and 2005, most of whom were young Black women and all of whom were sex workers. No one had a clue. Little got away with it for as long as he did not only because he was a drifter and killed randomly, but also because he went after the perfect prey. What's really interesting is that his killing activity peaked in the 1970s, the same time that Mr. Bundy was dominating the headlines.

And Little is by no means an anomaly:

* Charles Ng, from Hong Kong, abducted, raped, tortured, and killed between 11 and 25 women in Northern California in the mid-eighties.

* Derrick Todd Lee, an African American man, killed at least six women in Baton Rouge, Louisiana between 1992 and 2003.

* Coral Eugene Watts, an African American man, who is thought to have killed anywhere between 14 to 100 victims before finally being caught in 1982.

* Ángel Maturino Reséndiz, a Mexican native, murdered at least 23 people during the nineties before turning himself in.

* Rory Conde, a Colombian man, was responsible for six sex worker homicides, again in the nineties, in Miami, Florida.

We already saw with Gary Heidnik and Jeffrey Dahmer how the "right" victim selection can keep a killer going for years. During our research on these two killers, we came across the documentary *Killers for Company*. This film made a comparison between Heidnik and Dahmer, and while there is an obvious similarity—in that they were both white men targeting minorities in the eighties—that's about it. Dahmer was busy killing and creating his horrific male "sex zombies" in Wisconsin, while Heidnik was spending his time pilfering money, starting a church, and murdering Black women in Philadelphia. A much better comparison would be between serial killer Harrison Graham (a.k.a. the Corpse Collector) and Gary Heidnik, as proposed by Allan Branson from the University of Leicester in his study "African American Serial Killers: Over-Represented Yet Underacknowledged."

During the 1980s, the city of Philadelphia became the hunting ground for three killers: The Frankford Slasher—an unknown killer who starting in 1985 is suspected to have killed up to nine women over a period of five years. It was widely reported that all the victims were seen shortly before their disappearance with a middle-aged white man who was described as having "a round face, glasses, and a limp."

Then there was of course Gary Heidnik, who we had the pleasure of meeting in his basement earlier in this chapter. Finally, there was Harrison Graham, or as he was also known, Marty. Both Heidnik and Graham lured vulnerable, poor Black women, sometimes sex workers, to their houses where they held them captive. So the victimology is the *same*. And guess what? He lived just three miles down the road from Heidnik and was caught just a few months later.

But while Heidnik went on to become a pop culture muse as the inspiration for Buffalo Bill, there is not even a single book out there on Graham.

Maybe you're thinking, *OK, but we just went through Heidnik's crimes and even if he only killed two people, it was pretty shocking and sensational.* Well, I'd reserve your judgment on that until you read what Harrison Graham got up to. In fact, if we go by the FBI's definition of a serial killer—a killer who has killed three or more victims with defined cooling off periods in between—then Heidnik, who killed two women, isn't technically even a serial killer at all. Graham, on the other hand, killed seven people(!), and yet he is barely talked about. We're not saying let's turn him into a super-star, too, but we do need to talk about him, and his victims, so let's do that.

It was a scorching summer day in Philadelphia on Sunday, August 9, 1987 when the police started receiving phone calls from residents of a dere-lict-looking apartment building at 1631 North 19th Street. It was on a rough side of town with boarded up shops. News reports from the time suggest that it was a place of poverty, teeming with drugs, and the sound of sirens filled the air most days. The police weren't keen to head down there, but the residents were adamant. There was an unbearable stench coming from an apartment—it smelled like death.

In his book *Hunting Humans*, Michael Newton touches upon Harri-son Graham, and describes how when the police arrived they found that the door to the apartment had been nailed shut. This, along with the suffo-cating smell, immediately raised some eyebrows. Once inside, Officer Pete Scallatino found piles and piles of rubbish everywhere, half empty boxes of food, moldy magazines, and layers of human and dog feces. It was dis-gusting, but it wasn't the source of the putrefying stench, so he carried on deeper into the hovel.

Officer Scallatino eventually made it to the bedroom and there on the floor were the rotting bodies of two Black women. Investigators started sifting through the mountains of trash that filled the house, looking for more bodies, and bingo. Wrapped in sheets, hidden under mattresses and in cupboards, the police found six rotting corpses in total that day. The following day they found the remains of another body that no one had noticed on the roof of the building.

Police were quickly informed that a 28-year-old man named Harrison "Marty" Graham, had been living in that apartment for four years and just that month had left after an argument with the landlord. But people were surprised—Graham was a pretty chill guy and everyone liked him. The hunt for Graham was on, but he was a man used to keeping a low profile and avoiding attention and so he proved hard to track down. Meanwhile investigators were doing their best to identify Graham's seven victims; one of the bodies was that of Mary Jeter Mathis; 36, a local mother of five, and another body was that of Graham's own former girlfriend, Robin DeShazor; 29.

Finally, after eight days, Graham turned himself in and confessed to the seven murders; he had called his mother to ask for help and she had persuaded her son to stop running and just come home. Graham gave a 10-page confession, in which he admitted to police that he had lured his victims to his place with offers of drugs and money in exchange for sex, and then after sex he would murder them and hide them in his apartment.

Graham only seemed to show remorse for the killing of his ex-girlfriend, Robin DeShazor, saying; "I wanted so badly to love her, but I could not stop my need to do the other things. I never liked the sex and it got so much easier when I didn't have to see her . . . I didn't want her looking at me that way and I saw God being angry through her eyes."

In April 1988, Graham was convicted on seven counts of first-degree murder and seven counts of abusing a corpse. He was sentenced to life in prison and six death sentences.

As you can see, continuing to ignore marginalized victims is tragic, and ignoring non-white serial killers is dangerous. One of the main issues related to the lack of coverage of Black serial killers is not just that they are sidelined compared to their white counterparts, but that their very existence is erased. Under this kind of invisibility cloak, Black serial killers can hunt undetected and thereby kill already marginalized victims with impunity. As a society, we need to recalibrate our empathy gaps to make room for the less-dead.

SEX

Torture Trailers, Tribal Tats, and Truth or Consequences

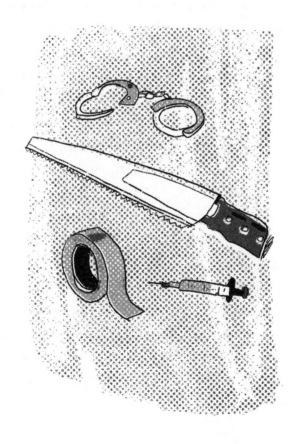

SEX, SEX, SEX, SEX, SEX. MOST OF US SPEND AN INORDINATE amount of time, money, and effort trying to get some. And even if the whole men-think-about-sex-every-seven-seconds thing isn't quite true, there's no denying that sex is everywhere from toothpaste commercials to true crime. We are a society *obsessed with sex.*

Sex, and the pursuit of it, is one of the few things we do as a species that weaves its way into every aspect of who we are: culturally, societally, physically, spiritually, biologically, and emotionally. Some would even go so far as to say that sex is our very raison d'etre; as if we're here to do nothing more than to just pass on our genes before we shuffle off our mortal coils. Whether or not we want to agree with that rather bleak, purely biological outlook, sex is absolutely one of our most powerful motivators as human beings. *(Let's be real—it's the reason we pay to get our pubes ripped out by a stranger every six weeks.)*

So perhaps it's no surprise then that a 2019 study, "Sex Differences in Serial Killers," found that 75 percent of male serial killers were motivated by sex.

In this chapter we're going to explore what happens when sex becomes intertwined with violence, aggression, and pleasure in the mind of a killer, and how this deadly combination has produced some of the most brutal and horrific offenders imaginable. We really have saved the very *worst* for last, so prepare yourselves. But before we step into a horrifying world of nightmarish torture dungeons to try and understand how sexual desire drives a *killer*, we need to first look at how sex and arousal impact the bodies and brains of us normal non-murderers. So get set to get wet—let's talk about sex, baby!

Your Brain on Sex

When we're turned on or having sex, our brains go into complete *overdrive*. Our neural reward centers light up like a sexy Christmas tree and our brains are flooded with a powerful cocktail of tasty, tasty chemicals like vasopressin, epinephrine, oxytocin, serotonin, and dopamine.

In 2003, the rather saucily titled study "Brain Activation During Human Male Ejaculation" found that during arousal and orgasm, blood flow to the cerebellum (the part of the brain that processes emotions) increases significantly, *but* the lateral orbitofrontal cortex (the center of logical reasoning, and the section of the brain responsible for rational decision-making) *completely* shuts off. So with our brain's logic center silenced and our emotional and thrill-seeking side screaming with euphoria, it's easy to see why we get carried away in the heat of the moment. And the huge surge of neurotransmitters like dopamine (the same chemical that gets people high when they take drugs like cocaine) explains why sex is so incredibly powerful, and even addictive.

Now obviously all this only happens when it's sex we *like*, and what we *like* can vary massively. And although the 2019 annual Pornhub report *(yes this does exist, and yes, we did look it up)* showed that the most common search terms on their site were *lesbian, threesome, big tits,* and *milf,* it would appear that most of us are not quite as vanilla as all that. Because according to a 2011 study, "How Unusual Are the Contents of Paraphilias?," a whopping 64 percent of men surveyed reported a sexual interest in at least one paraphilia.

What's a *paraphilia*? We're glad you asked. It's defined by the American College of Psychiatrists as "any intense and persistent sexual interest other than sexual interest in genital stimulation or preparatory fondling with

phenotypically normal, physically mature, consenting human partners."
Basically, someone with a paraphilia is turned on by objects, activities, situations, and targets that are considered abnormal when connected to sex. Check out our paraphilia sidebar to discover the turn-ons you aren't likely to see in the latest edition of *Cosmo*.

PARAPHILIAS YOU NEVER ASKED FOR, BUT WILL NEVER BE ABLE TO FORGET

Here are some of the most *interesting* paraphilias we came across:

Agalmatophilia: arousal from statues, mannequins, and immobility.

Autoplushophilia: sexual arousal caused by oneself dressed as a giant, cartoon-like stuffed animal.

Climacophilia: experiencing erotic gratification by falling down stairs.

Coprophilia: a sexual fixation with feces.

Dacryphilia: sexual arousal brought about by the sight of tears.

Infantilism: sexual arousal from acting like and being treated as a baby.

Klismaphilia: sexual gratification from enemas.

Maschalagnia: a sexual attraction to armpits.

Partialism: sexual fixation with one part of the human body, like a foot.

Plushophilia: a sexual interest in stuffed animals.

Telephone scatologica: talking dirty to a total stranger on the phone who is not expecting it.

Urophilia: a sexual fixation with urine.

As odd as some of us may find certain paraphilias, they are a very personal thing. And if you're not hurting yourself or anyone else, *why not* crawl around dressed up like a baby, or whip out that mannequin leg and have at it? According to the *DSM-5*, a paraphilia *only* becomes a diagnosable *paraphilic disorder* when:

* the person with the paraphilia feels distressed about their sexual interests (and not just because of society's judgey-ness)

* their sexual desire or behavior causes another person's psychological distress, injury, or death

* their desire for sexual behaviors involve unwilling targets unable to give legal consent, for example, children, animals, or corpses

If someone with a paraphilic interest in children, animals, or corpses were to act on their sexual interests in the UK, all three would be criminal offenses. In the US whether bestiality or necrophilia is a crime varies quite *significantly* from state to state. Why, exactly, bestiality has been illegal in Virginia since 1661 but only illegal in Vermont since 2017, and as of 2021 it's still not illegal in Wyoming, is beyond us. If you want to know why Washington was forced to introduce bestiality laws in 2006, check out our horsey sidebar on page 198.

WHY THE LONG WAIT TO CRIMINALIZE FUCKING A HORSE?

Did you know that bestiality was not illegal in the State of Washington from 1975 until 2006? It had previously been covered under the same set of laws that outlawed sodomy, but those were repealed in 1975 to decriminalize consensual, homosexual, or heterosexual sex acts involving adult humans.

But if lawmakers thought they could just forget about the animals they were wrong. Bestiality was once again made illegal in Washington after the now notorious Enumclaw case. We really don't want to get into the details, but basically a man decided to break into a farm in the city of Enumclaw in King County, Washington, and forced a horse to have sex with him. Turns out this wasn't a great idea at all, and he died shortly afterward from some quite serious internal injuries. We know exactly what happened to him, though, because he had actually filmed the entire thing to distribute as part of his bestiality porn collection . . .

But anyway! The *DSM-5* differentiates between paraphilias that are just seen as a bit weird and those that cause some sort of distress or harm. For the latter, it specifically lists eight such disorders:

1. **Exhibitionistic disorder:** exposing oneself or doing sexual things in front of other people

2. **Fetishistic disorder:** recurrent, intense sexual arousal from use of an inanimate object or from a very specific focus on a non-genital body part (or parts) that causes significant distress or functional impairment

❸ Frotteuristic disorder: touching or rubbing someone who does not want to be touched or rubbed against with your genitals

❹ Pedophilic disorder: recurrent intense sexually arousing fantasies, urges, or behaviors involving prepubescent or young adolescents, usually under the age of 13

❺ Transvestic disorder: recurrent intense sexual arousal from cross-dressing, or dressing as the opposite gender, and in which that person's urge to do so causes significant distress or impairment in their daily life

❻ Voyeuristic disorder: getting off by watching an unsuspecting person who is disrobing, naked, or engaged in sexual activity

❼ Sexual masochism disorder: recurring and intense sexual arousal in response to enduring moderate or extreme pain, suffering, or humiliation

❽ Sexual sadism disorder: experiencing persistent and intense sexual arousal from causing or fantasizing about the physical or mental suffering of another person, with or without their consent

As you can see, it's quite the list—it is controversial—and the discussion of any of these conditions would no doubt give us a fascinating insight into the realm of human behavior and sexual desire. But in this chapter, we are going to focus on that last disorder—sexual sadism—and how killers operating with this particular paraphilia are the epitome of absolute nightmare fuel when it comes to true crime.

And it's not just us who think so. Sexually sadistic serial killers are, as former FBI agent Robert Hazelwood called them in his 1990 paper "The Sexually Sadistic Criminal and His Offenses," "the most dangerous, destructive, elusive, brutal, and cunning of all aberrant offenders."

But before we get into it, let's make one thing clear—when we're talking about sexually sadistic offenders, we're *not* talking about BDSM culture.

Sexual Sadism

Sadism and masochism—when carried out within the confines of a consenting BDSM relationship between adults, using safe words, boundaries and agreements—is of course completely A-OK. Get the locks, get the paddles, get the blindfolds, and go for it!

And while it's true that those who take part in such sexual activities as doms may very well be sexual sadists, it doesn't mean that they have sexual sadism *disorder*—and it certainly doesn't mean that they're killers. Sexual sadism, like most things, exists on a spectrum, and for some the consensual role-play of BDSM is all they need to get their kicks.

Sexually sadistic offenders and killers, though, unlike the regular folk of the kink community, live out their sadistic sexual fantasies on other people *without* consent. They act with the direct aim of gratifying themselves and enhancing their own sexual arousal from observing the pain, humiliation, terror, torture, and even death of their victim. These guys are a very *specific* group of twisted individuals. The reason we're making such a big deal about definitions is not just because we're annoying and super anal, but also because of something else we need to clarify: not all sex offenders are sexual sadists.

As we mentioned at the start of this chapter, 75 percent of male serial killers are motivated by sex, but research carried out by psychiatrist Dr. Richard Kruger in 2010 found that of the thousands and thousands of sex offenders in US prisons, roughly *only* 10 percent were full-blown sexual sadists.

How does that work? I hear you ask. *Surely* all *rapists are sadists?* Well, no; all rapists are *despicable,* but as explained by psychiatrist Dr. Allen J. Frances in his 2012 paper "Sexual Sadism: Avoiding Its Misuse in Sexually Violent Predator Evaluations," they are not all sadists.

To understand this, we need to distinguish between physical cruelty used during the commission of a crime like rape and murder, and sadism. An opportunistic rapist, for example, will resort to violence and murder if needed to get what he wants. He may have *biastophilia,* a paraphilia in which sexual arousal is dependent on the act of assaulting a non-consenting person, whereas the sexual sadist intentionally and methodically tortures the victim for the sole purpose of self-sexual arousal.

Trying to wrap our heads around what makes this kind of killer tick is deeply unpleasant; we know that. But it's vital to understanding *why* they do what they do. To really try and get inside the head of a sexual sadist, we think the best way is to follow the guidance of criminologist Dr. Lee Mellor, as described on his podcast *Murder Was the Case.*

So, take a second and think about your own sexual fantasy . . . Go on . . .

Back with us? Good. Now, we're guessing that a big part of your fantasy was not just what you were doing to someone, but also *their* response to it—the look on their face; the sounds they were making; how they were responding to you. This is a vital part of everyone's sexual fantasies.

For sadists, they want to see fear, pain, and humiliation—*that's* what turns them on. And if their victim stopped responding to the violence (i.e., stopped screaming in terror and pain), the sadist would stop being aroused. They would then escalate the torture and brutality in order to restart their captive's fear response so that they could reach sexual gratification.

We know it's a lot to take in, but check out our sidebar where we examine the "sexually sadistic cycle" Dr. Mellor describes to see how this works.

SEXUAL SADISM'S CYCLICAL CIRCUS

In an episode on sexual sadists on his podcast *Murder Was the Case*, Dr. Lee Mellor describes the cycle that a sexually sadistic offender traps his victim in:

STEP 1, Infliction of negative stimuli: This is the act of the torture itself.

STEP 2, Watching the reaction of fear, terror, and humiliation: This step is what *actually* delivers the sexual sadist their sexual kick. Sexual gratification for the sadist does not come from step 1, but rather from *seeing* the reaction of their victim to the horrible thing they are doing.

STEP 3, Experience of feeling an enhanced self-concept: This stage is the existential kick; the sadist feels better about themselves. They enjoy their feeling of superiority and they want to inflict more pain to keep getting the rush and thrill from steps 2 and 3.

Escalation

The cycle of torture and pleasure is addictive for a sexually sadistic offender. Just like how our non-murder-y brains light up when we're given the right sexy stimuli, the sadist's brain (which seems to have its wires crossed between pain and sex) goes into overdrive at the sight and sound of fear. The 2012 study "Increased Fronto-temporal Activation During Pain Observation in Sexual Sadism" even revealed that sexual sadists differ from non-sadists at a *neurological* level when it comes to witnessing pain in others. This study found that sexual sadists showed increased activity in the left amygdala (the brain's reward center) in response to pictures of pain, whereas non-sadists did not.

We'll come back to exploring what is going on in the brain of a sexual sadist later in this chapter. For now, what we need to focus on is that once the sadist gets into this cycle, they want to sustain their sexual high, and it hooks them like a drug. And just like with a drug, the sadist also starts to develop a tolerance to others' pain and suffering. Soon they find that they need an increasingly heightened reaction from a victim in order to get the same sexual kick. This is when we start to see the torture *intensify*.

With sexual sadists, once they move from fantasy to hands-on offending, their path of perversion will only get more destructive. Their acts of sexual sadism will grow increasingly bizarre and violent over time. And although sexual sadists are not necessarily primarily motivated by murder—because they want a living victim to extract pleasure from—their insatiable sexual attraction to sadistic behavior, and their often rapid escalation in search of that sexual high, usually leads them to kill.

Some of the most notorious sexual sadists include Andrei Chikatilo (a.k.a. the Rostov Ripper); Dennis Rader (a.k.a. BTK); Bob Berdella (a.k.a.

the Kansas City Butcher); Peter Kurten (a.k.a. the Vampire of Dusseldorf); and Robin Gecht and the Ripper Crew of Chicago.

All these men are examples of truly ghoulish killers, and they all make us to want to hide in our houses forever. But over at *RedHanded* HQ, we've decided that there is one offender who stands whips and chains above the rest; one person who scared the fuck out of us like no one else. David Parker Ray (a.k.a. the Toy Box Killer) has invaded more of our post-research nightmares and sent more chills down our spines than any other criminal we have ever encountered in all the years we've been neck-deep in true crime. *(Which is really fucking annoying because you know he'd just have bloody loved that!)*

David Parker Ray, as you are about to discover, symbolizes the sexually sadistic psychopath better than anyone else. In 2001 he was sentenced to 224 years in prison for a string of horrendous abductions, and although he was never actually convicted of murder, this was *not* due to a lack of brutality or an insufficient number of women vanishing around him. Despite the fact that they never found the bodies, the FBI and the New Mexico State Police remain absolutely convinced that Ray is indeed a serial killer who most likely murdered upwards of 50 victims, gaining him his nickname the Toy Box Killer.

David Parker Ray: Scrap Metal Sex Toys

On March 22, 1999, residents of the New Mexican town of Elephant Butte *(and yes, that is the actual name of the actual town)* were horrified to see a woman covered in blood, running down the street screaming for help. She was completely naked except for a large metal collar wrapped around her neck connected to a six-foot chain that was dragging behind her.

When the police arrived, the woman, who had taken refuge in an elderly couple's home, told them that her name was Cynthia Vigil Jaramillo and that she had been held captive, tortured, and raped by the couple who lived at 513 Bass Road. The police sent a patrol car to the address while they took Cynthia to the nearest hospital. Once her injuries had been seen to and the collar had been removed from around her neck, Cynthia Jaramillo told the police her harrowing story . . .

She was a sex worker and three days earlier she had been standing in a parking lot in Albuquerque waiting for business. It was then that she was approached by a man who offered her $20 for oral sex. Cynthia agreed and went with him to his parked RV. Once in the vehicle, the john told Cynthia that he was actually an undercover police officer and that she was under arrest for solicitation. This man was of course none other than David Parker Ray—and he was *not* a policeman.

Straight away we see Ray start to tick the classic boxes of a homicidal sexual sadist. They tend to follow a very specific pattern of behaviors, and one of the most common—according to forensic psychologist Dr. J. Reid Meloy—is impersonating law enforcement in the commission of an offense. So, check.

As we continue with this disturbing story, you'll see a macabre game of pervert bingo unfolding with regards to the other key traits. Check out the full list in our sidebar on page 206.

TRAITS-OF-THE-SEXUALLY-SADISTIC-KILLER
BINGO

Above average intelligence.	Commits crimes that are carefully planned and well thought out.	Murdered victim is concealed.
A history in the military and an attraction to jobs in policing.	Rape almost always leads to murder.	Offender records his activities meticulously.
Socially adept; uses his charisma and personality to lure the victim.	Abduction of victim to a pre-selected location.	Attack is methodical and repeated from one victim to another.
Has a partner who assists with the offenses.	Emotional detachment during attacks.	Rehearsal fantasy is a prerequisite.

With Cynthia now handcuffed and restrained in the back of the motorhome, Ray and his girlfriend Cindy Hendy *(you really couldn't make these names up)*, who had been hiding in the RV, started the 150-mile drive back to Elephant Butte. Once they arrived at 513 Bass Road, Cynthia was forced into the house and led through the couple's house of horrors at gunpoint. Her blood froze as she saw that each room was filled with more bizarre and horrific-looking torture devices than the last.

After the nightmare tour was over, Cynthia was tied up and a tape recording started to play. It was Ray's calm, cold voice, and the tape started with "Hello there, bitch."

The Tape

Now, we simply cannot include a full transcript of what was said on that tape in this book because it would take up at least 20 pages, and because you'd probably be sick. So we'll break it down for you and give you the SparkNotes version condensed from the court transcripts.

On the recording Ray explains to his captive that she has been abducted and is being kept prisoner for his sexual pleasure and for that of "his lady." He states that the tape was made on July 23, 1993, a full six years before Cynthia Vigil Jaramillo was taken, and he confirms that he has been kidnapping women for years. The listener is then told that she will be kept like an animal—fed, watered, cleaned, and allowed to use the bathroom—but that she will be shown no mercy and that she will not like what is about to happen to her.

In his chillingly matter-of-fact voice, Ray then drones on *(as if he's making an instructional tape for a new employee at McDonalds)* saying that the captive will be trained to tolerate pain, raped multiple times a day, and made to perform oral sex on both him and his lady. He calls this process his "enlightening crash course in sex." Then like some deranged Bond villain, Ray explains to his hostage what he calls his "safe method of disposal:" he tells her he will inject her with a combination of sodium pentothal and phenobarbital and this will leave her with no memory of what had been done to her. If she causes trouble, though, he says he'll kill her.

Ray then gives a detailed list of what he likes and what he doesn't, and warns his victim that if she gets it wrong she will be punished with electric shocks. He even describes a metal frame that he would strap his victims into so that they would be totally immobile while they were raped by him, his mates, and his dog. Yes, you read that right: his dog.

Then in a bizarre twist, the victim is then told that she will be made to fill in a medical questionnaire, answering questions like how many children she has and when she last menstruated. Finally, the tape ends with: "Be smart and be a survivor. Don't talk without permission. Be very quiet, and by all means, show proper respect. Have a nice day."

This straight-outta-*Saw* audio was just one piece of horrendous evidence that police found at 513 Bass Road, but going back to our sadist traits from page 206, we can see that this tape reveals how Ray ticks yet more boxes on this nightmare list. He clearly engaged in a hell of a lot of detailed rehearsal fantasy (the recording of the tape itself tells us that). He was extremely meticulous in his planning (this will become even more obvious once we enter the "toy box"). And he clearly repeated a highly methodical approach from victim to victim (the police found stacks of those medical questionnaires indicating years of countless victims).

What's also interesting to note is that Ray has an accomplice (yet more bingo!), but this "lady" he refers to on the tape can't be Cindy Hendy. They didn't meet until 1998, six years *after* the tape was made. But for now, let's get back to Cynthia.

The Ice(pick) Capades

The horror of the tape she had just heard was only the beginning of Cynthia's torment. As outlined in the book *Slow Death* by James Fielder, after the recording finished she was chained to a bed in the living room and repeatedly electrocuted while Ray calmly photographed the entire ordeal. He then sat down next to Cynthia and presented her with a series of photographs showing numerous other women who had endured the same fate. As we can see from the tape and this disgusting little trip down memory lane, Ray got off on the psychological torment of his victims in the same way he enjoyed their physical pain.

The next morning, Ray left for work and Cindy Hendy was left to keep watch over Cynthia. For a while she did a good job, but as the morning wore on—perhaps getting complacent since Cynthia *was* chained to the wall— Hendy's vigilance started to wane. Just after lunchtime, the house phone rang and Hendy wandered off to answer it, leaving the keys to the collar around Cynthia's neck on a nearby coffee table.

Cynthia could hardly believe it. Trying to make as little noise as possible, she carefully pulled the table toward her using her feet. Once it was close enough, she grabbed the keys and undid the padlock that connected the chain around her neck to the wall. But then Hendy came back into the living room, grabbed a lamp, and smashed it over Cynthia's head. As Cynthia desperately felt around on the floor, trying to find anything to fight back, her hands found an ice pick; she swung it up and sliced the back of Cindy Hendy's head. *(The fact that there was an ice pick just lying around in the living room tells you a lot about the setup at 513 Bass Road.)*

With Hendy now on the ground clutching her head wound, Cynthia made a break for it. And that's how she ended up running through Elephant Butte totally naked with a collar around her neck and trailing a six-foot metal chain.

Having heard Cynthia's horror story, Elephant Butte police headed out to find David Parker Ray and Cindy Hendy. Surprisingly, the pair proved pretty easy to track down—not only is Elephant Butte a very small place, but Ray and Hendy weren't exactly laying low. In fact, they were driving around town looking for their escaped captive.

When police pulled over their RV, Ray tried to tell them that Cynthia was a crazy heroin addict who they had actually been helping. He claimed that he and Cindy Hendy *had* chained Cynthia up in their house, but it was only to get her through the worst days of drug withdrawal. But the police, seeing the massive gash on Cindy Hendy's head, weren't buying their good-Samaritan-chain-you-to-the-wall drug rehab center story, and promptly arrested the pair. Within days both were charged with assault, kidnapping, conspiracy, and unlawful penetration.

Before we go into what happened next and what exactly the police discovered at 513 Bass Road, we need to go back in time to pay David Parker Ray's childhood a little visit.

Finger-Painting BDSM

David Parker Ray was born in 1939 in Belen *(and you have no idea how much we want to add a "d" to the end of that town name! Non-Brits who are confused: "bell end" should definitely be a part of your swears arsenal, look it up!),* New Mexico, a small town just south of Albuquerque. His parents divorced when he was young, and he and his sister Peggy ended up living with their paternal grandfather. Granddad Ray wasn't exactly a kindly old Werther's Original–type; he was a big fan of extreme physical discipline.

Little David was also regularly visited by his alcoholic father, who would spend their time together savagely beating his son and then "make up for it" by giving him his old BDSM magazines. These hand-me-down porno mags soon became young David's escape from a homelife filled with abuse, and a school life marred by relentless bullying. Slowly, he started to retreat socially and began spending all his time immersed in a world of glossy pictures depicting bondage, punishment, and sex.

His other hobby was arts and crafts, but it wasn't exactly stick-it-on-the-fridge material. Ray became obsessed with drawing images of violent sex acts, and he even started a scrapbook that he filled with magazine clippings of the BDSM positions he was particularly drawn to. This early exposure to such extreme sexual content sparked a lifelong fascination in Ray with sadism, and by the age of 14 he discovered that he wasn't able to get any sexual satisfaction unless he was fantasizing about someone in serious pain. No one in his life seemed to notice or care that he was quite evidently displaying some majorly worrying signs.

Formation of a Sexual Sadist

So what can Ray's story tell us about how a sexually sadistic killer is created? Well, like with most cases we have discussed so far, there are both genetic and environmental factors involved. According to most studies—including one we looked at in chapter 2 called "The Incidence of Child Abuse in Serial Killers" by Heather Mitchell and Michael Aamodt—the main form of abuse that correlates to the development of sexually sadistic killers is childhood psychological abuse. It is thought that the emotional trauma and anxiety of the abuse interferes with a child's usual psychosexual development, disturbing the standard pattern of arousal and accidentally linking it with violence, fear, and suffering.

Essentially for these individuals during childhood and adolescence, as their sexuality is developing, violence and sexual pleasure become enmeshed. How exactly this happens is not *that* well understood, clinically speaking, but there are a few theories. Many of these theories build on an idea posed in 1990 by sexologist John Money, who suggested that sexual sadism is like a disease that destroys the center of the brain relating to sexual arousal—the amygdala, hippocampus, and hypothalamus—and that it hijacks the pathways of the brain related to sexual arousal, like the limbic system. This results in the brain sending out messages about sex and violence *at the same time*, crossing these two wires in a super dangerous way.

There is also evidence to suggest that physical abnormalities in an individual's brain can be a contributing factor, and numerous studies, such as the 1995 paper "Offender and Offense Characteristics of Sexual Sadists," by T. Gratzer and J. M. Bradford, have found that most sexual sadists showed damage to their right temporal horn, a part of the brain that contributes to emotional processing.

There are many ways that sexual sadism can develop, and it's not always caused by abuse or trauma; it could just come down to differences in brain structure. Sadism also exists on a spectrum. While some people can just be into BDSM and manage their sexually sadistic tendencies that way, it seems that the most *catastrophic* results from sexual sadism arise when the sadist also has an antisocial personality disorder like our old friend all the way from chapter 1—psychopathy.

Although the roots of sexual sadism aren't yet fully understood, what is *known* is that such offenders usually start to have violent sexual fantasies as young children and begin to act on these thoughts in early adult life. Once they start there is very little chance of them stopping—and their behavior invariably ends in murder.

Now with that out of the way, let's get back to David Parker Ray and his next tick on the sexually sadistic killer bingo card: a career in the military. Ray had been in the Army for a few years before he was eventually honorably discharged, and during his time in the service he became quite the mechanic. This skill served him well throughout his life; not only did he land a mechanic job at the state park in Elephant Butte, but it meant that he could also make all manner of the hellish mechanical torture devices to use on his victims.

Not that anyone would have known it. Because again, just as Dr. Meloy's list of traits predicts, Ray was highly charming and was well liked in Elephant Butte. All his colleagues at the state park had nothing but nice things to say about him, and he was famous for throwing big parties, especially on Halloween.

This is one of the characteristics that make sexually sadistic offenders the ultimate predators—they are often respected within their communities; they hold down steady jobs; they are high functioning with high IQs; and they are much more socially intelligent than other offenders. This makes them able to blend in and operate effectively without suspicion. This all meant that people were initially shocked to discover that Ray had been arrested, and the small-town gossip mill spun into a blur as Cynthia Jaramillo's story spread like wildfire.

Not all the locals were surprised, however, and the police received a tip from a local couple who were close with Cindy Hendy. They claimed that one night about a month before, Hendy got drunk and told them that she and Ray had abducted and tortured a woman named Angela before pumping her full of drugs and dropping her off on I-25. Hendy had also told her friends that her boyfriend was a serial killer.

Apparently, the couple had just brushed it all off as a drunken story, which gives us a disturbing glimpse into their social circle, but OK. And while the tip was something, it wasn't like they would be able to track down this random Angela. Well, as it turned out, she would find *them*.

On March 27, a woman named Angelica Montano turned up at 513 Bass Road to tell the police every detail of her ordeal at the hands of Ray and Hendy. If anyone suspected Angelica of being an attention seeker, those thoughts were quickly shot down when the deputy sheriff of a nearby town claimed that he had actually picked up a hitchhiking Angelica on I-25 about a month before, and during the two hours she was in his car on their way to Albuquerque she had told the deputy sheriff the same exact story. Long before Cynthia Jaramillo had ever been abducted.

The "Toy Box": Satan's Caravan

By this point, the police and the FBI had been searching the house and the trailer in the garden for 10 days, and given what they had found, they knew that there were likely dozens if not hundreds of other victims.

In the house, every single wall had been plastered with images of graphic pornography, and while most of us might have artwork or ornaments we've collected hanging up around the place, this house was full of whips, chains, and motorized torture devices. The police even found "sex toys" that seemed to have been made out of old scrap metal.

What was especially odd was that while all of this overtly sexual and morbid paraphernalia was proudly displayed out in the open, some other things were carefully hidden away. Investigators discovered a large collection of jewelry, name badges, watches, and other trinkets concealed in a secret box. There were more than four hundred unique items in this odd menagerie, and given that these items didn't seem to belong to Ray or Hendy, for investigators this set off major trophy-keeping, serial-killing alarm bells.

Things only got worse when Ray's diaries were discovered. It appeared that he kept incredibly detailed and ordered accounts of every single assault he had ever committed *(meticulous record-keeping bingo)*. According to these journals, many of the women he abducted had died as a result of what he had done to them. The problem for investigators was that he never included his victims' names in these torture logs, so tracking them down or matching them to missing persons' accounts would be difficult if not impossible.

I wish I could say that all of this craziness was the worst of it, but I'm afraid it's not even close. The time has come for us to finally head into the toy box. The 15-by-25-foot white trailer in the backyard of 513 Bass Road looked pretty innocuous from the outside, and despite all that investigators had found in the house, no one was prepared for what lay inside. On March 17, 1999, the Elephant Butte police and the FBI opened up the trailer.

In the middle of the trailer sat a large gynecological chair complete with stirrups. The walls were covered in steel leg spreaders, a homemade breast stretcher, electric shock machines, pulleys, straps, syringes, clamps, surgical scalpels, saws, and a collection of enormous dildos. There was even a giant sign that said "Satan's Den" and another that read, "If she's worth taking, she's worth keeping." *(Suddenly "Live, Laugh, Love" doesn't seem so bad.)*

As investigators stood there taking it all in, they also noticed to their horror that there was a mirror on the ceiling. It was positioned so that the person in the chair could see absolutely everything that was being done to them. The police soon discovered that the "toy box" was almost totally soundproof and that there were CCTV cameras and motion sensors placed strategically inside and outside this hellish torture caravan.

Vials of sodium pentothal and phenobarbital were also found in the trailer. Just like Ray had stated in his "welcome" tape, these drugs seem to have been used to fog up his victims' memories. Both drugs can be lethal if a person is given too much, and with Ray not exactly being medically trained—and given how many victims his diaries point to—it seems highly likely to us that he almost certainly killed some of the women he brought into his "toy box."

At this point things were looking bad for David Parker Ray and his girl-friend accomplice Cindy Hendy, but the police needed *more*—they needed to find more victims, dead or alive. Because once he was confronted with the contents of his torture caravan toy box, Ray simply claimed that any of the women who were ever there had been willing participants. Even if you are happy to ignore Cynthia and Angelica's stories that they were most definitely *not* there willingly, you have to ask yourself why he was drugging them all then? If it had all been so consensual, why did he need to try and make the women forget what had happened?

The many questions this case gives rise to are never likely to be answered, though; sexually sadistic offenders are some of the most difficult for law enforcement to interview. Former FBI agent Robert Hazelwood went so far as to call them "worthy adversaries," stating that they will not cooperate or reveal anything even when faced with overwhelming evidence and that victims would be unlikely to come forward out of shame, so ex-girlfriends would be the best way to discover the truth. *(Keep those bingo markers on hand, because we have a full house to get to.)*

Cindy Hendy didn't care about keeping quiet. She knew she was done for; she had been actively involved in the abductions, torture, and sexual assaults of Cynthia Jaramillo and Angelica Montano, so she decided to try and save herself by giving the police everything she had on her boyfriend. She explained that Ray would pick up sex workers, usually ones who had substance abuse issues, bring them back to the house, and torture them for days.

Once he was done, sometimes he would inject them full of drugs and let them go, but sometimes if they caused too much trouble, he would kill them. Hendy claimed that he would either open up the victim's chest cavity and fill it with rocks before driving out to Elephant Butte Lake to dump the body, or he would just go over to Texas and ditch the remains in the desert.

This was way more information than the police had expected from

Hendy, but they were stuck; Elephant Butte Lake is enormous (it can hold 2,065,010 acre-feet of water!) and there was no way they could search it all. As for the vague description of a Texas desert, it was not much use either. But Hendy was adamant that Ray was a killer, and she told police that she believed he had been killing for his entire adult life. Apparently he had revealed to Hendy that his first kill was at age 20, and that after this he had never looked back. Eventually the police tracked down Ray's four ex-wives, and they too claimed that he had confessed to them about killing women since his early twenties.

According to Hendy, Ray had killed at least 30 people, and his diaries corroborated this. The problem was that Hendy claimed Ray had never shown her a single body dump site, so she couldn't pinpoint any locations to the authorities. To us this makes sense; we don't think that Ray would have been dumb enough to reveal to Hendy where he disposed of the bodies. For many power-obsessed sexual serial killers, where they leave their victims becomes a secret they cherish and happily take to their grave.

Hendy also revealed that Ray kept meticulous photo diaries of his conquests, but that he would periodically burn them, just in case. Again, we think all this completely adds up. Ray was incredibly detail-oriented and he took careful steps to avoid detection, like drugging his victims. Although he kept photos and records, he never recorded any of his victims' names, and destroying evidence as he went shows the classic traits of a highly intelligent and organized offender.

Worse Than Weatherspoons:
Blue Water Saloon

Although not much of what Hendy told the police panned out, she did turn the authorities onto another person of interest—a man named Dennis Yancy. Hendy told police that Yancy and Ray had tortured and killed Yancy's ex-girlfriend, a woman named Marie Parker.

Parker had been a 22-year-old mother of two when she disappeared without a trace in 1997 from a bar in Elephant Butte called the Blue Water Saloon. Her ex, Dennis Yancy, was a real piece of work. At just 27 years old he had already been convicted of numerous counts of domestic violence and rape. Yancy had ended up hanging out with Ray because of their shared interest in Satanism and sadism.

The police brought Yancy in for questioning and he admitted that he and Ray would pick up sex workers and torture them together in the toy box. He also eventually admitted that on the 4th of July weekend in 1997, he had taken Parker from the bar to Ray's house and handed her over to him. Parker had been kept prisoner by Ray for days before Yancy claimed that he was forced to strangle his ex-girlfriend to death.

Apparently, Ray photographed the whole thing and then the two of them drove Parker's body out into the desert and left her in a ravine in Monticello Canyon. Parker's body has never been found. Despite this, Yancy was convicted of murder in the second degree and sentenced to 25 years. No one else has ever been charged with the murder of Marie Parker and there isn't much the police can do without a body.

Tribal Tattoos Sometimes
Aren't a Terrible Idea

If you thought this story was over, we still have more to come . . . so buckle up. The FBI was able to pull footage from the CCTV that had been set up inside the toy box, and there was one particular section of film that had been taped in July 1996 that caught their attention. It showed a woman restrained in the gynecological chair with her legs strapped into the stirrups and David Parker Ray doing unspeakable things to her. The footage wasn't clear enough to identify the woman's face, but there was one distinguishing feature that was picked up by the cameras.

The woman had a distinctive tattoo on her left calf; it is often described as a "tribal swan." Even in the nineties—the era of the tribal tattoo—the police thought it was so unusual that surely someone would recognize it. And as it turns out, they were right.

A woman came forward from the nearby town of Truth or Consequences. *(Yes, that is the name of the town. Apparently it used to be called Hot Springs, which is a much less terrifyingly ominous name, but the townsfolk decided to change it in 1950 to celebrate the 10-year anniversary of a popular radio quiz show of the same name. Because why the hell not?)*

But anyway, the woman with the tribal swan tattoo was a former local named Kelli Van Cleave, and in July 1996 she had gone missing for three days after a night out at—you guessed it—the Blue Water Saloon. She had been there with a young woman named Jesse Ray, and Jesse was the very own daughter of Mr. David Parker Ray. Kelli had no memory of what had happened to her that night or in the three days following, but since that incident Kelli had been terrified of duct tape and would have recurring nightmares of being strapped to a table.

The FBI brought Jesse Ray in for questioning; it seemed like too much of a coincidence that the last person to have been with Kelli before she ended up strapped to David Parker Ray's torture chair was his own daughter. They strongly suspected that Jesse was involved, but unlike everyone else, Jesse Ray kept her mouth shut during her interrogations—not that this helped her much after Cindy Hendy, desperate for a plea deal, outed Jesse as an accomplice. The FBI eventually charged Jesse Ray with kidnapping and criminal sexual penetration. She pleaded no contest and received a 30-month sentence. (No contest means that you still claim you are innocent, but accept that the state has enough evidence to convict you.)

After an arduous series of legal proceedings, in February 2000 David Parker Ray finally pleaded guilty to all charges associated with Cynthia Vigil Jaramillo, and on September 20, 2001, David Parker Ray was sentenced to 223 years in prison. But he was not a well man, and in 2002, just eight months into his sentence, he died of a massive heart attack. To this day, New Mexico law enforcement and the FBI remain convinced that David Parker Ray's many victims lie scattered across the desert and at the bottom of Elephant Butte Lake.

Human remains were even found in the lake in 1999, but with no DNA samples of suspected victims to test, there's no way of knowing who it was. One of the main questions people ask about the case of David Parker Ray is why he set any of his victims free, but again to us, this fits with the profile of a sexual sadistic offender. Most studies on these killers show that they are not usually motivated directly by the kill—they enjoy the torture—but their constant need for escalation and the way they lose control once they are aroused lead to murder. Unlike with necrophiles, the dead body of their victim is collateral damage to be swiftly disposed of, not the endgame.

Everything about Ray indicates that he was highly committed to what he was doing; he spent years and over $100,000 building his toy box—and he did not want to get caught. He knew that racking up bodies would attract unwanted attention and also create a load of extra work for him, so he developed his "safe disposal method"; that way he could be confident that his victims wouldn't remember enough to lead back to him.

Ray also picked women he knew wouldn't be believed even if they *did* remember anything. Angelica Montano had told a deputy sheriff what had happened to her a month before Cynthia Jaramillo was taken, but he didn't believe her and he did nothing. By attacking the less-dead, Ray didn't even need to kill them to get what he wanted.

Finally, we also think that David Parker Ray liked the control of knowing that the women, while they may not remember everything, would know that *something* horrendous had happened to them. Ray definitely got a thrill out of psychological torture, so we think for him just knowing that those women were out there living with the fear and pain of the unknown was deeply satisfying to his sexually sadistic mind.

Conclusion

AT THE START OF THIS BOOK WE ASKED YOU TO COME ON A journey with us to examine the various factors that can set a person on the path to violence, criminality, and murder. We warned you that despite delving into some of the most reprehensible and aberrant acts imaginable, we wouldn't be discussing monsters, but people.

So, what makes a killer tick? The only logical answer then is lots of things. It's a perfect, or should we say *imperfect,* storm. There is no definitive reason. A killer can spring from an abusive childhood, a genetic makeup, and a personality disorder all working together at once. There is no pathology unique to a killer; rather, killers are the culmination of genetics, experienced trauma, environmental factors, society, culture—*everything* that makes us human.

Where does that leave the rest of us? We've talked a lot in this book about what makes a *killer* tick, but what makes *us* tick when it comes to our fascination with killers? From serial killers to family annihilators and the seemingly out-of-the-blue murders featured on *Snapped,* we're hooked.

Now of course, a fascination with killers is something that exists on a spectrum—from reading this book and listening to *RedHanded* the podcast all the way up to buying yourself a John Wayne Gacy clown painting or purchasing a strand of Richard Ramirez's hair. *(Yes, some people do take it that far.)*

There's a crime fanatic in all of us, and even though people like to say that true crime is just so *hot and mainstream* right now, there's nothing new about it. Victorian media moguls realized in 1888 how much better their newspapers sold when Jack the Ripper had been out and about. They churned out weekly illustrated Penny Dreadfuls featuring grisly, sensationalist stories of murder and the macabre, filling up their greedy coffers and satisfying the morbid masses. And the commercial crime consumption never stopped.

The American true crime writer Harold Schechter calls our collective fascination with murder, and with serial killers in particular, "a kind of cultural hysteria." But what is it rooted in? To us it feels like the story of killers is the story of our own deepest fears—the fear that something may happen to us, or possibly even a loved one, at the hands of a stranger. And the even more insidious dread that we may be capable of hurting someone else—and what that would really mean for us.

Humanity has always been obsessed with fear; we're biologically hard-wired for it. If our first ancestors hadn't known fear in the face of a razor-toothed Smilodon, we as a species certainly wouldn't have lasted long. We are obsessed with fear and death, and our obsession with true crime is a sort of *controlled* fear. Perhaps it just gives us a little boost of delicious dopamine or maybe it makes us feel more prepared for if we were ever to find ourselves in a dangerous situation. Or even, as artist and serial killer memorabilia collector Joe Coleman explained in an interview with the BBC in 2016, "It's a cathartic way of releasing the demons in a way that's positive rather than destructive."

As true crime podcasters and authors, we are asked in almost every interview, ever: Why are people obsessed with true crime? This idea of true crime being a kind of catharsis, although controversial, is probably the best one out there. Perhaps our fascination with killers is actually an outlet for us to play out in our minds our darkest and most disturbing thoughts, and thereby sweep them away afterward without having acted on them. Maybe.

We also think that cultural historian and author of *The Red Barn Murder*, Shane McCorristine, explained the timeless nature of true crime fascination best when he said that it is an "opportunity to suffer death from a distance, to get as close to the abyss as you can while not falling in."

And serial killer Dennis Nilsen agrees. Many passages from Nilsen's prison diaries were published in the 1985 book *Killing for Company* by Brian Masters, and one extract in particular stood out to us:

> Their [meaning, us] fascination with 'types' (rare types) like myself plagues them with the mystery of why and how a living person can actually do things which may be only those dark images and acts secretly within them. I believe they can identify with these 'dark images and acts' and loathe anything which reminds them of this dark side of themselves.

Killers aren't mythical monsters we can other-ize and just ignore. They are an amplification of our worst impulses. They are a projection of our darkest fascinations. Killers are—as is the true crime genre itself—the perfect mirror to hold up to society to reveal who we really are. Whatever the reason, true crime allows us to plumb the depths of human depravity, explore our deepest fears, get right up against it, then simply close the book and walk away. After we have read about the very worst things one human can do to another, we can shake off the shivers and go back to our everyday lives lying on the sofa, watching *90 Day Fiancé*, and eating peanut butter straight out of the jar.

But before you close *this* book, take a second to think about all that we have discussed over the past several pages and ask yourself: If crime is a reflection of our society, what does our obsession with violent killers say about us?

Bibliography

Chapter 1: Genetics

Adams, Tim. "How to Spot a Murderer's Brain." *Guardian*. May 11, 2013. https://www.theguardian.com/science/2013/may/12/how-to-spot-a-murderers-brain.

Awe, Lynne. *Who Are They? The Psychopath and The Serial Killer Personality – Differences, Detection and Diagnosis*. Phoenix: Argosy University, 2012.

Barras, Colin. "The Controversial Debut of Genes in Criminal Cases." BBC.com. May 30, 2018. https://www.bbc.com/future/article/20180530-the-controversial-debut-of-genes-in-criminal-cases.

Blair, R. J. R., and D. G. V. Mitchell. "Psychopathy, Attention and Emotion." *Psychological Medicine* 39, no. 4 (2009): 543–55. https://doi.org/10.1017/S0033291708003991.

Bonn, Scott A. "The Differences Between Psychopaths and Sociopaths." *Psychology Today*. January 9, 2018. https://www.psychologytoday.com/gb/blog/wicked-deeds/201801/the-differences-between-psychopaths-and-sociopaths.

Brunner, H. G. "MAOA Deficiency and Abnormal Behavior: Perspectives on an Association." *Ciba Foundation Symposium* 194 (1996): 155–164. https://doi.org/10.1002/9780470514825.ch9.

Cleckley, Hervey M. *The Mask of Sanity: An Attempt to Clarify Some Issues About the So-Called Psychopathic Personality*, 2nd edition. Martino Fine Books, 2014.

Cook, Gareth. "Secrets of the Criminal Mind." *Scientific American*. May 7, 2013. https://www.scientificamerican.com/article/secrets-criminal-mind-adrian-raine/.

Dingman, M. "Know Your Brain: Prefrontal Cortex." Neuroscientifically Challenged. May 17, 2014. https://www.neuroscientificallychallenged.com/blog/2014/5/16/know-your-brain-prefrontal-cortex.

Esposito, L. and D. Devilly. "The Psychopathy Checklist." Clintools.com. http://www.clintools.com/victims/resources/assessment/personality/psychopathy_checklist.html.

Fallon, James. "How I Discovered I Have the Brain of a Psychopath." *Guardian.* June 2, 2014. https://www.theguardian.com/commentisfree/2014/jun/03/how-i-discovered-i-have-the-brain-of-a-psychopath.

Fallon, James. *The Psychopath Inside: A Neuroscientist's Personal Journey into the Dark Side of the Brain.* New York: Portfolio, 2013.

Fallon, Jim. "Exploring the Mind of a Killer." TED video. July 16, 2009. https://www.youtube.com/watch?v=u2V0vOFexY4

Foulkes, L., E. J. McCrory, C. S. Neumann, and E. Viding. "Inverted Social Reward: Associations Between Psychopathic Traits and Self-Report and Experimental Measures of Social Reward." PLoS ONE 9, no. 8 (2014). https://doi.org/10.1371/journal.pone.0106000.

Fox, B. and M. DeLisi. "Psychopathic Killers: A Meta-Analytic Review of the Psychopathy-Homicide Nexus." *Aggression and Violent Behaviour* 44 (2019): 67–79. https://doi.org/10.1016/j.avb.2018.11.005.

Godar, S. C., P. J. Fite, K. M. McFarlin, and M. Bortolato. "The Role of Monoamine Oxidase A in Aggression: Current Translational Developments and Future Challenges." *Progress in Neuro-Psychopharmacology & Biological Psychiatry* 69 (2016): 90–100.

https://doi.org/10.1016/j.pnpbp.2016.01.001.

Grohol, John M. "Differences Between a Psychopath vs Sociopath." PsychCentral. February 12, 2015. https://psychcentral.com/blog/differences-between-a-psychopath-vs-sociopath#1.

Hare, Robert D. *Manual for the Revised Psychopathy Checklist*, 2nd ed. Toronto: Multi-Health Systems, 2003.

Hare, Robert D. and C. N. Neumann. "The PCL-R Assessment of Psychopathy: Development, Structural Properties, and New Directions." In *Handbook of Psychopathy*, edited by C. Patrick, 58–88. New York: Guilford, 2006.

Hare, R. D., & S. D. Hart. "Psychopathy, Mental Disorder, and Crime." In *Mental Disorder and Crime*, edited by S. Hodgins, 104–115. Thousand Oaks, CA: SAGE, 1993.

Hercz, Robert. "Psychopaths Among Us." Hare.org. http://www.hare.org/links/saturday.html#:~:text=Yes%2C%20almost%20all%20serial%20killers,calls%20them%20%22subclinical%22%20psychopaths.

Horgan, John. "Code Rage: The 'Warrior Gene' Makes Me Mad! (Whether I Have It or Not)." *Scientific American*. April 26, 2011. https://blogs.scientificamerican.com/cross-check/code-rage-the-warrior-gene-makes-me-mad-whether-i-have-it-or-not/.

Hunter, P. "The Psycho Gene." *EMBO Reports* 11, no. 9 (2010): 667–669. https://doi.org/10.1038/embor.2010.122.

Jewell, Tim and Timothy Legg. "Sociopath." Healthline. September 28, 2018. https://www.healthline.com/health/mental-health/sociopath.

Khan, Nadia and Wendy Boring-Bray. "Psychopath vs. Sociopath: The Telltale Signs & Difference." Betterhelp.com. December 21, 2020. https://www.betterhelp.com/advice/sociopathy/psychopath-vs-socio-path-the-telltale-signs-differences.

Koenigs, M. "The Role of Prefrontal Cortex in Psychopathy." *Reviews in the Neurosciences* 23, no. 3 (2012): 253–262. https://doi.org/10.1515/revneuro-2012-0036.

Larson, Erik. *The Devil in the White City*. New York: Crown Publishing Group, 2002.

LeDoux, J. "Know Your Brain: Amygdala." Neuroscientifically Challenged. June 24, 2014. https://www.neuroscientificallychallenged.com/blog/know-your-brain-amygdala.

Lindberg, Sara and Timothy Legg. "Psychopath." Healthline. January 9, 2019. https://www.healthline.com/health/psychopath#signs.

Martens, Willem H. J. "The Hidden Suffering of the Psychopath." *Psychiatric Times*. October 7, 2014. https://www.psychiatrictimes.com/view/hidden-suffering-psy-chopath.

McCullough, Jack. "The Psychopathic CEO." *Forbes*. December 9, 2019. https://www.forbes.com/sites/jackmccullough/2019/12/09/the-psychopathic-ceo/.

McDermott, R., D. Tingley, J. Cowden, G. Frazzetto, and D. Johnson. "Mono-amine Oxidase A Gene (MAOA) Predicts Behavioral Aggression Following Provocation." *PNAS* 106, no. 7 (2009): 2118-2123. https://doi.org/10.1073/pnas.0808376106.

Merriman, T. and V. Cameron. "Risk-taking: Behind the Warrior Gene Story." *New Zealand Medical Journal* 120 (2007). http://hdl.handle.net/10822/510354.

Mestel, Rosie. "Does the 'Aggressive Gene' Lurk in a Dutch Family?" *New Scientist.* October 30, 1993. https://www.newscientist.com/article/mg14018970-600-does-the-aggressive-gene-lurk-in-a-dutch-family.

Meyer, J. H., N. Ginovart, A. Boovariwala, S. Sagrati, D. Hussey, A. Garcia, T. Young, N. Praschak-Rieder, A. A. Wilson, and S. Houle. "Elevated Monoamine Oxidase A Levels in the Brain: An Explanation for the Monoamine Imbalance of Major Depression." *Archives of General Psychiatry* 63, no. 11 (2006): 1209–1216. https://doi.org/10.1001/archpsyc.63.11.1209.

Motzkin, J., J. Newman, K. Kiehl, and M. Koenigs. "Reduced Prefrontal Connectivity in Psychopathy." *Journal of Neuroscience* 31, no. 48 (2011) 17348–17357. https://doi.org/10.1523/JNEUROSCI.4215-11.2011.

Myers, W. C., E. Gooch, and J. R. Meloy. "The Role of Psychopathy and Sexuality in a Female Serial Killer." *Journal of Forensic Sciences* 50, no. 3 (2005): 652–657. https://doi.org/10.1520/JFS2004324.

Ohikuare, Judith. "Life as a Nonviolent Psychopath." *The Atlantic.* January 21, 2014. https://www.theatlantic.com/health/archive/2014/01/life-as-a-nonviolent-psychopath/282271/.

O'Driscoll, K., and J. P. Leach. "No Longer Gage": An Iron Bar Through the Head. BMJ 317, no. 7174 (1998): 1673–1674. https://doi.org/10.1136/bmj.317.7174.1673a.

Pomeroy, Ross. "Can Psychopaths Be Cured?" Real Clear Science. July 10, 2014. https://www.realclearscience.com/blog/2014/07/can_psychopaths_be_cured.html.

Purse, Marcia and Daniel B. Block. "How Sociopaths Are Different from Psychopaths." Verywell Mind. June 15, 2020. https://www.verywellmind.com/what-is-a-sociopath-380184.

Raine, Adrian. *The Anatomy of Violence: The Biological Roots of Crime.* New York: Penguin, 2013.

Robinson, Kara Mayer and Joseph Goldberg. "Sociopath v. Psychopath: What's the Difference?" WebMD. August 24, 2014. https://www.webmd.com/mental-health/features/sociopath-psychopath-difference.

Romero-Rebollar, C., F. Ostrosky-Shejet, B. Camarena-Medellín, M.A. Bobes-León, K.X. Díaz-Galván. "Effect of MAOA Promoter Polymorphism and Neuropsychological Performance on Psychopathy Traits." *Revista Médica Del Hospital General De México* 78, no. 1 (2015): 21–26. https://doi.org/10.1016/j.hgmx.2015.03.004.

Selzer, Adam. *H. H. Holmes: The True History of the White City Devil*, illustrated edition. New York: Skyhorse, 2017.

Smith, Cary Stacy, and Li-ching Hung. *Subclinical Psychopaths: How They Adapt, Their Interpersonal Interactions with and Effect on Others, and How to Detect Them*. Springfield, IL: Charles C Thomas, 2013.

Sohrabi, S. "The Criminal Gene: The Link Between MAOA and Aggression (REVIEW)." *BMC Proceedings* 9, A49 (2015). https://doi.org/10.1186/1753-6561-9-S1-A49.

Sterbenz, Christina. "Why Norway's Prison System Is So Successful." Business Insider. December 11, 2014. https://www.businessinsider.com/why-norways-prison-system-is-so-successful-2014-12?r=US&IR=T

Stone, M. H. "Serial Sexual Homicide: Biological, Psychological, and Sociological Aspects." *Journal of Personality Disorders* 15, no. 1 (2001): 1–18. https://doi.org/10.1521/pedi.15.1.1.18646.

Tuvblad, C., S. Bezdjian, A. Raine, and L. A. Baker. "The Heritability of Psychopathic Personality in 14- to 15-year-old Twins: A Multirater, Multimeasure Approach." *Psychological Assessment* 26, no. 3 (2014):704-716. https://doi.org/10.1037/a0036711.

Viding, Essi. "Why Do Some People Become Psychopaths?" (lecture, The Royal Society, London, October 19, 2017). https://royalsociety.org/science-events-and-lectures/2017/10/rosalind-franklin/.

"Why Do People Commit Murder?" ACS Distance Education. https://www.acs.edu.au/info/behaviour/behavioural-disorders/psychopaths-and-murderers.aspx.

Yong, Ed. "Dangerous DNA: The Truth About the 'Warrior Gene.'" *New Scientist*. April 7, 2010. https://www.newscientist.com/article/mg20627557-300-dangerous-dna-the-truth-about-the-warrior-gene/.

Chapter 2: Childhood and Adolescence

Barker, Eric. "Interview with FBI Profiler Jim Clemente." Barking Up the Wrong Tree. October 2013. https://www.bakadesuyo.com/2013/10/fbi-profiler/.

Benecke, M. "Two Homosexual Pedophile Sadistic Serial Killers: Jurgen Bartsch (Germany, 1946–1976) and Luis Alfredo Garavito Cubillos (Colombia, 1957)." *Journal of Psychology & Psychotherapy* 7, no. 5 (2017). https://www.researchgate.net/publication/271848016_Two_homosexual_pedophile_sadistic_serial_killers_Jurgen_Bartsch_Germany_1946_-_1976_and_Luis_Alfredo_Garavito_Cubillos_Colombia_1957.

Bonn, Scott A. *Why We Love Serial Killers: The Curious Appeal of the World's Most Savage Murderers.* New York: Skyhorse, 2014.

Bonn, Scott A. "The Zodiac and Other Thrill Killers." *Psychology Today.* September 21, 2015. https://www.psychologytoday.com/gb/blog/wicked-deeds/201509/the-zodiac-and-other-thrill-killers.

Bretherton, I. "The Origins of Attachment Theory: John Bowlby and Mary Ainsworth." *Developmental Psychology* 28, no. 5 (1992): 759–775. https://doi.org/10.1037/0012-1649.28.5.759.

Brody, Paul. *Son of Sam: A Biography of David Berkowitz.* Golgatha, 2016.

Brückweh, Kerstin. "Fantasies of Violence. German Citizens Expressing Their Concepts of Violence and Ideas about Democracy in Letters Referring to the Case of the Serial Killer Jürgen Barts (1966-1971)." *Crime, Histoire & Sociétés / Crime, History & Societies* 10, no. 2 (2006): 53-81. http://www.jstor.org/stable/42708653.

The Dangerous Few. Documentary film. 2018. https://www.youtube.com/watch?v=auQc9_wb76Y.

"Gilles de Rais: History's First Serial Killer?" In *Encyclopedia Brittanica.* https://www.britannica.com/story/gilles-de-rais-historys-first-serial-killer.

Greene, Melissa Fay. "30 Years Ago, Romania Deprived Thousands of Babies of Human Contact." *The Atlantic.* June 30, 2020. https://www.theatlantic.com/magazine/archive/2020/07/can-an-unloved-child-learn-to-love/612253/.

Krupić, D., S. Ručević, and S. Vučković. "From Parental Personality over Parental Styles to Children Psychopathic Tendencies." *Current Psychology* (2020). https://doi.org/10.1007/s12144-020-00676-6.

Marono, A., S. Reid, E. Yaksic, and D. Keatley. "A Behaviour Sequence Analysis of Serial Killers' Lives: From Childhood Abuse to Methods of Murder." *Psychiatry, Psychology and Law* 27, no. 1 (2020) 126–137. https://doi.org/10.1080/13218719 .2019.1695517.

Marshall, John J. "Aaron Campbell: Some Social Workers in Denial about Child Psychopaths." *Scotsman.* April 2, 2019. https://www.scotsman.com/news/ opinion/columnists/aaron-campbell-some-social-workers-denial-about-child-psychopaths-dr-john-j-marshall-1420786.

Mitchell, H. and M. Aamodt. "The Incidence of Child Abuse in Serial Killers." *Journal of Police and Criminal Psychology* 20, no. 1 (2015): 40-47. https://doi. org/10.1007/BF02806705.

Moor, Paul. *Jürgen Bartsch: Selbstbildnis eines Kindermörders.* Rowohlt-Taschen-buch-Verlag, 2003.

Murderers and Their Mothers. Television series. Featuring Elizabeth Yardley. Released May 16, 2016. https://www.cbsreality.tv/uk/shows.php?title=murder-ers+and+their+mothers.

Nolen, Jeannette L. "Bobo Doll Experiment." In *Encyclopedia Britannica.* Article published October 6, 2009. https://www.britannica.com/event/Bobo-doll-ex-periment.

Norris, J. *Serial Killers.* Smithfield, NSW: Gary Allen, 2002.

Ressler, Robert K. and Tom Shachtman. *Whoever Fights Monsters.* New York: St. Martin's, 2002.

Tymula, A., L. Rosenberg Belmaker, A. Roy, L. Ruderman, K. Manson, P. Glimcher, and I. Levy. "Adolescents' Risk-taking Behavior Is Driven by Tolerance to Ambiguity." *Proceedings of the National Academy of Sciences* 109, no. 42 (2012): 17135-17140. https://doi.org/10.1073/pnas.1207144109.

Walker, Shaun. "Thirty Years On, Will the Guilty Pay for Horror of Ceaușescu Orphanages?" *Guardian.* December 15, 2019. https://www.theguardian.com/ world/2019/dec/15/romania-orphanage-child-abusers-may-face-justice-30-years-on.

Zeanah, C., N. Fox, and C. Nelson. "The Bucharest Early Intervention Project." *Journal of Nervous and Mental Disease* 200, no. 3 (2012): 243–247. https:// doi.org/10.1097/NMD.0b013e318247d275.

Chapter 3: Insanity

American Psychiatric Association. *Diagnostic and Statistical Manual of Mental Disorders: DSM-5*, 5th edition. Washington, DC: American Psychiatric Publishing, 2013.

Asokan, T. V. "Daniel McNaughton (1813–1865)." *Indian Journal of Psychiatry* 49, no. 3 (2007): 223–224. https://doi.org/10.4103/0019-5545.37328.

Carey, Benedict. "Are Mass Murderers Insane? Usually Not, Researchers Say." *New York Times*. November 8, 2017. https://www.nytimes.com/2017/11/08/health/mass-murderers-mental-illness.html.

Charatan, F. "Mother Who Drowned Her Five Children Is Granted a Retrial After Witness Gave False Evidence." *BMJ* 330, no. 112 (2005). https://doi.org/10.1136/bmj.330.7483.112-b

Eftimiades, Maria. *Sins of the Mother*. New York: St. Martin's, 1995.

Evans, Gareth. "How Credible Are Lie Detector Tests?" *BBC News*. October 4, 2018. https://www.bbc.co.uk/news/world-us-canada-45736631.

Feuerstein, S., F. Fortunati, C. A. Morgan, V. Coric, H. Temporini, and S. Southwick. "The Insanity Defense." *Psychiatry (Edgmont)* 2, no. 9 (2005): 24–25.

Lati, Marisa. "She Captivated the Nation by Saying a Black Man Kidnapped Her Sons. Police Knew She Killed Them." *Washington Post*. October 25, 2019. https://www.washingtonpost.com/history/2019/10/25/she-captivated-nation-by-saying-black-man-kidnapped-her-sons-police-knew-she-killed-them/.

McLellan, Faith. "Mental Health and Justice: The Case of Andrea Yates." *Lancet* 368, no. 9551 (2006): 1951–1954. https://doi.org/10.1016/s0140-6736(06)69789-4.

Miller, Laurence. *Criminal Psychology*. Springfield: Charles C Thomas, 2012.

Mugshots. "A Mother's Madness: Andrea Yates." Television episode. Aired October 28, 2002.

Pogrebin, M., R. Regoli, and K. Perry. "Not Guilty by Reason of Insanity: A Research Note." *International Journal of Law and Psychiatry* 8, no. 2 (1986): 237–241. https://doi.org/10.1016/0160-2527(86)90038-5.

"Postpartum Psychosis." 2021. NHS. https://www.nhs.uk/conditions/post-partum-psychosis/.

"Preacher Said He Tried to Save Yates' Family." ABC News. March 27, 2002. https://abcnews.go.com/GMA/story?id=126222&page=1.

Smith, David. *Beyond All Reason*. New York: Kensington, 1995.

Spencer, Suzy. *Breaking Point*. New York: Diversion, 2002.

Chapter 4: Misogyny

Baker, Peter C. "Hunting the Manosphere." *New York Times*. June 13, 2017. https://www.nytimes.com/2017/06/13/magazine/hunting-the-manosphere.html.

Barbaro, Michael. "Listen to 'The Daily': Mental Health and Mass Shootings." *New York Times*. February 23, 2018. https://www.nytimes.com/2018/02/23/podcasts/the-daily/gun-access-mentally-ill.html.

Beauchamp, Zack. "Incel, the Misogynist Ideology That Inspired the Deadly Toronto Attack, Explained." Vox. April 25, 2018. https://www.vox.com/world/2018/4/25/17277496/incel-toronto-attack-alek-minassian.

Bosman, Julie, Kate Taylor, and Tim Arango. "A Common Trait Among Mass Killers: Hatred Toward Women." *New York Times*. August 10, 2019. https://www.nytimes.com/2019/08/10/us/mass-shootings-misogyny-dayton.html.

Cecco, Leyland. "Toronto Van Attack Suspect Says He Was 'Radicalized' Online by 'Incels.'" *Guardian*. September 27, 2019. https://www.theguardian.com/world/2019/sep/27/alek-minassian-toronto-van-attack-interview-incels.

Duriesmith, David, Shannon Zimmerman, and Luisa Ryan. "Recognizing the Violent Extremist Ideology of Incels." *Women in International Security Policy Brief*. September 2018. https://www.academia.edu/37532571/Recognizing_the_Violent_Extremist_Ideology_of_Incels.

Franco, Joseph. "Preempting Incel-Inspired Violent Extremism in Asia." Australian Institute of International Affairs. July 30, 2020. https://www.internationalaffairs.org.au/australianoutlook/preempting-incel-inspired-violent-extremism-in-asia/.

Hoffman, Bruce and Jacob Ware. "Incels: America's Newest Domestic Terrorism Threat." *Lawfare*. January 12, 2020. https://www.lawfareblog.com/incels-americas-newest-domestic-terrorism-threat.

"Incels (Involuntary Celibates)." Anti-Defamation League. 2021. https://www.adl. org/resources/backgrounders/incels-involuntary-celibates.

Lewis, Helen. "To Learn About the Far Right, Start With the 'Manosphere.'" *The Atlantic*. https://www.theatlantic.com/international/archive/2019/08/anti-feminism-gateway-far-right/595642/.

Manne, Kate. *Entitled: How Male Privilege Hurts Women*. New York: Crown, 2020.

Oxford English Dictionary. Oxford: Oxford University Press, 2015.

Springer, Andrew. "The Secret Life of Elliot Rodger." ABC News. 2015. https://abcnews.go.com/US/fullpage/secret-life-elliot-rodger-24322227.

Tolentino, Jia. "The Rage of the Incels." *New Yorker*. May 15, 2018. https://www. newyorker.com/culture/cultural-comment/the-rage-of-the-incels.

Wright, Jennifer. "Why Incels Hate Women." *Harper's Bazaar*. April 27, 2018. https://www.harpersbazaar.com/culture/politics/a20078774/what-are-incels/.

Chapter 5: Cults

American Psychiatric Association. "Cautionary Statement for Forensic Use of DSM-5." In *Diagnostic and Statistical Manual of Mental Disorders: DSM-5*, 5th edition. Washington, DC: American Psychiatric Publishing, 2013.

Bainbridge, William Sims and Rodney Stark. "Cult Formation: Three Compatible Models." *Sociology of Religion* 40, no. 4 (1979): 283–295. https://doi. org/10.2307/3709958.

Belief: The Possession of Janet Moses. Documentary film. Directed by David Stubbs. Netflix. Released July 27, 2015. https://www.netflix.com/title/80126016.

"Borderline Personality Disorder." Mind. 2021. https://www.mind.org.uk/information-support/types-of-mental-health-problems/borderline-personality-disorder-bpd/about-bpd/.

"Borderline Personality Disorder." National Institute of Mental Health. 2021. https:// www.nimh.nih.gov/health/publications/borderline-personality-disorder/index. shtml.

Butler A. C., G. Brown, A. T. Beck, and J. R. Grisham. "Assessment of Dysfunctional Beliefs in Borderline Personality Disorder." *Behaviour Research & Therapy* 40, no. 10 (2002): 1231–1240. https://doi.org/10.1016/s0005-7967(02)00031-1.

Collins, Glenn. "The Psychology of the Cult Experience." March 15, 1982. *New York Times*. https://www.nytimes.com/1982/03/15/style/the-psycholo-gy-of-the-cult-experience.html.

Conroy, J. Oliver. "An Apocalyptic Cult, 900 Dead: Remembering the Jonestown Massacre, 40 Years On." *Guardian*. November 17, 2018. https://www.theguard-ian.com/world/2018/nov/17/an-apocalyptic-cult-900-dead-remembering-the-jonestown-massacre-40-years-on.

Goodman, Felicitas D. *The Exorcism of Anneliese Michel*, illustrated edition. Resource Publications, 2005.

Guinn, Jeff. *The Road to Jonestown: Jim Jones and Peoples Temple*. New York: Simon & Schuster, 2018.

Jonestown: Terror in the Jungle. Documentary miniseries. Directed by Shan Nich-olson and Richard Lopez. Storyville for the BBC, 2020. https://www.bbc.co.uk/programmes/p07y21yw.

Kaplan, David E. and Andrew Marshall. *The Cult at the End of the World*. New York: Crown, 1996.

Latson, Jennifer. "The Jonestown Massacre Remembered." *Time*. November 18, 2014. https://time.com/3583781/jonestown-massacre/.

Lester D. "The Role of Irrational Thinking in Suicidal Behavior." *Comprehensive Psychology* 1, no. 8 (2012). https://doi.org/10.2466/12.02.07.16.CP.1.8.

Metraux, Daniel. *Aum Shinrikyo and Japanese Youth*. Lanham, MD: University Press of America, 1999.

"Overview: Borderline Personality Disorder." NHS. July 17, 2019. https://www.nhs.uk/mental-health/conditions/borderline-personality-disorder/overview/.

Reiterman, Tim. *Raven: The Untold Story of the Rev. Jim Jones and His People*. New York: Tarcher Perigee, 2008.

Salande, J. D. and D. Perkins. "An Object Relations Approach to Cult Membership." *American Journal of Psychotherapy* 65, no. 4 (2011): 381–391. https://doi.org/10.1176/appi.psychotherapy.2011.65.4.381

Scheeres, Julia. *A Thousand Lives: The Untold Story of Jonestown*. New York: Simon & Schuster, 2012.

Yardley, E., D. Wilson, and A. Lynes. "A Taxonomy of Male British Family Annihilators." *The Howard Journal of Criminal Justice* 53, no 2 (2014): 117–140. https://doi.org/10.1111/hojo.12033.

Chapter 6: Relationships

Arrigo, B. A. and A. Griffin. "Serial Murder and the Case of Aileen Wuornos: Attachment Theory, Psychopathy, and Predatory Aggression." *Behavioral Sciences and the Law*, 22 (2004): 375–393. https://doi.org/10.1002/bsl.583.

Barr, G. A., S. Moriceau, K. Shionoya, K. Muzny, P. Gao, S. Wang, and R. M. Sullivan. "Transitions in Infant Learning Are Modulated by Dopamine in the Amygdala." *Nature Neuroscience* 12 (2009): 1367–1369. https://doi.org/10.1038/nn.2403.

Champagne, F. A. and M. J. Meaney. "Transgeneration Effects of Social Environment on Variations in Maternal Care and Behavioral Response to Novelty." *Behavioral Neuroscience* 121, no. 6 (2007): 1353–1363. https://doi.org/10.1037/0735-7044.121.6.1353.

Cheney, M. *The Co-Ed Killer: A Study of the Murders, Mutilations, and Matricide of Edmund Kemper* III. Goodreads Press, 2017. Kindle.

Chesney-Lind, Medna. *The Female Offender: Girls, Women, and Crime*. Thousand Oaks: SAGE, 1998.

Cresswell, Kim. *Edge of Madness: The Story of Joseph Kallinger*. KC Publishing, 2017.

Davis, Carol A. *Couples Who Kill*. Allison & Busby, 2006.

Federoff, J. P., A. Fishell and B. Federoff. "A Case Series of Women Evaluated for Paraphilic Sexual Disorders." *The Canadian Journal of Human Sexuality* 8, no. 2 (1999): 127–140. https://www.thefreelibrary.com/A CASE SERIES OF WOMEN EVALUATED FOR PARAPHILIC SEXUAL DISORDERS.-a058410760.

Fox, James A. and Jack Levin. *The Will to Kill: Making Sense of Senseless Murder*, 3rd edition. Thousand Oaks: SAGE, 2006.

Friskics-Warren, M. K. HYBRISTOPHILIA 12. Boston: Allyn and Bacon, 1994.

Gaudenti, S. "Female Sex Offenders: Breaking the Mold the Hard Way." In *Sex Crimes & Paraphilia*, edited by E.W. Hickey, 361–367. Upper Saddle River, NJ: Pearson Prentice Hall, 2006.

Gavin, H. "Evil or Insane? The Female Serial Killer and Her Doubly Deviant Femininity." In *Transgressive Womanhood*, edited by M. Hedenborg White & B. Sandhoff, 49–60. Oxford: Inter-Disciplinary Press, 2014.

Glatt, John. *The Family Next Door: The Heartbreaking Imprisonment of the Thirteen Turpin Siblings and Their Extraordinary Rescue.* New York: St. Martin's, 2020.

Gurian, E.A. "Explanations of Mixed-sex Partnered Homicide: A Review of Sociological and Psychological Theory." *Aggression and Violent Behavior* 18, no. 5 (2013): 520–526. http://dx.doi.org/10.1016/j.avb.2013.07.007.

Hazelwood, R., J. Warren, and P. Dietz. "Compliant Victims of the Sexual Sadist." *Australian Family Physician* 22, no. 4 (1993): 474–479. https://pubmed.ncbi.nlm.nih.gov/8481110/.

Hickey, Eric. *Serial Murderers and Their Victims*, 7th edition. Cengage Learning, 2015.

Hoffman, Jan. "Do Serial Killers Just Stop? Yes. Sometimes." *New York Times*. April 26, 2018. https://www.nytimes.com/2018/04/26/health/serial-killers-golden-state.html.

Hofer, Myron A. *The Roots of Human Behavior*. San Francisco: W. H. Freeman, 1981.

Johnston, Joni E. "Partners in Crime." *Psychology Today*. January 20, 2014. https://www.psychologytoday.com/gb/blog/the-human-equation/201401/partners-in-crime#.

Keene, Louis. and Mathew Haag. "13 Siblings, Some Shackled to Beds, Were Held Captive by Parents, Police in California Say." *New York Times*. January 15, 2018. https://www.nytimes.com/2018/01/15/us/siblings-captive-california.html.

Krizan, Z. and A. D. Herlache. "The Narcissism Spectrum Model: A Synthetic View of Narcissistic Personality." *Personality and Social Psychology Review* 22, no. 1 (2018): 3–31. https://doi.org/10.1177/1088868316685018.

Lo, R. and J. Rosewood. *The Toolbox Killers: A Deadly Rape, Torture & Murder Duo*. CreateSpace Publishing, 2017.

MacKinnon, Catharine. *Toward a Feminist Theory of State*. Cambridge, MA: Harvard University Press, 1989.

Mann, C.R. *When Women Kill*. Albany: State University of New York, 1996.

Margaritoff, Marco. "Doreen Lioy Was a Successful Editor—But She Gave It All Up to Marry a Serial Killer." All That's Interesting. January 16, 2021. https://allthatsinteresting.com/doreen-lioy.

McGowan, P. O., A. Sasaki, A. C. D'Alessio, S. Dymov, B. Labonté, M. Szyf, G. Turecki, and M. J. Meaney. "Epigenetic Regulation of the Glucocorticoid Receptor in Human Brain Associates with Childhood Abuse." *Nature Neuroscience* 12, no. 3 (2009): 342–348. https://doi.org/10.1038/nn.2270.

Mina, Denise. "Why Are Women Drawn to Men Behind Bars?" *Guardian*. January 13, 2003. https://www.theguardian.com/world/2003/jan/13/gender.uk.

Moriceau, S. and R. M. Sullivan. "Maternal Presence Serves as a Switch Between Learning Fear and Attraction in Infancy." *Nature Neuroscience* 9, no. 8 (2006): 1004–1006. https://doi.org/10.1038/nn1733.

Money, John. *Lovemaps: Clinical Concepts of Sexual/Erotic Health and Pathology, Paraphilia, and Gender Transposition in Childhood, Adolescence, and Maturity*. New York: Prometheus, 1986.

Ramsland, Katherine. "Women Who Love Serial Killers." *Psychology Today*. April 20, 2012. https://www.psychologytoday.com/gb/blog/shadow-boxing/201204/women-who-love-serial-killers.

Ramsland, Katherine. "Mur-Dar, the Dark Side of the Sixth Sense." *Psychology Today*. February 26, 2014. https://www.psychologytoday.com/gb/blog/shadow-boxing/201402/mur-dar-the-dark-side-the-sixth-sense.

Rettner, Rachael. "Epigenetics: Definition & Examples." Live Science. June 24, 2013. https://www.livescience.com/37703-epigenetics.html.

Roth, T. L., F. D. Lubin, A. J. Funk, and J. D. Sweatt. "Lasting Epigenetic Influence of Early-Life Adversity on the BDNF Gene." *Biological Psychiatry* 57, no. 8 (2009): 823–831. https://doi.org/10.1016/j.biopsych.2008.11.028.

Schreiber, Flora. *The Shoemaker: The Anatomy of a Psychotic*. New York: Simon & Schuster, 1983.

Scott, H. The Female Serial Murderer: A Sociological Study of Homicide and the "Gentler Sex." Lampeter, Ceredigion, Wales: The Edwin Mellen Press, 2005.

Seeman, M. "Women Attracted to Incarcerated Men: A Case Study." *Journal of Patient Care* no 4 (2018): 139-141.   DOI: 10.4172/2573-4598.1000139.

Sharma, B. R. "Disorders of Sexual Preference and Medicolegal Issues Thereof." *American Journal of Forensic Medicine and Pathology* 24, no. 3 (2003): 277–282. https://doi.org/10.1097/01.paf.0000069503.21112.d2.

Shipley, Stacey L. and Bruce A. Arrigo. *The Female Homicide Offender: Serial Murder and the Case of Aileen Wuornos*. Upper Saddle River, NJ: Prentice Hall, 2004.

Siomopoulos, V. and J. Goldsmith. "Sadism Revisited." *American Journal of Psychotherapy* 30, no. 4 (1976): 631–640. https://doi.org/10.1176/appi.psychotherapy.1976.30.4.631.

Swart, Joan and Lee Mellor L. *Homicide: A Forensic Psychology Casebook*. Boca Raton, FL: CRC Press, 2017.

Sullivan, R. and E. N. Lasley. "Fear in Love." Dana Foundation. September 1, 2010. https://www.dana.org/article/fear-in-love/.

Sullivan, R. M., M. Landers, B. Yeaman, and D. A. Wilson. "Good Memories of Bad Events in Infancy: Ontogeny of Conditioned Fear and the Amygdala." *Nature* 407 (2000): 38–39. https://doi.org/10.1038/35024156.

Williams, Stephen. *Invisible Darkness: The Horrifying Case of Paul Bernardo and Karla Homolka*, 2nd edition. SDS Communications, 2013. E-book.

Woster, M. "Differences in Characteristics of Criminal Behavior Between Solo and Team Serial Killers." Dissertations. 463 (2020). Digital Commons @ NLU. https://digitalcommons.nl.edu/diss/463.

Chapter 7: Bigotry

Branson, Allan L. "African American Serial Killers: Over-Represented Yet Under-acknowledged." *Howard Journal of Criminal Justice* 52, no. 1 (2012): 1–18. https://doi.org/10.1111/j.1468-2311.2012.00731.x.

Englade, Ken. *Cellar of Horror: The Story of Gary Heidnik*. New York: St. Martin's, 1989.

The Grindr Serial Killer. Documentary film. BBC3. November 24, 2016. https://www.youtube.com/watch?v=iMPAKrwHmSg.

Landsberg, Mitchell. "Dahmer Case Raises Complaints of Racism with PM-Dahmer Confession, Bjt." AP News. 1992. https://apnews.com/article/6452017abebd-b9eaa87e90817bf59b7e.

Newton, Michael. *Hunting Humans: Encyclopedia of Modern Serial Killers*. New York: Avon, 1992.

Picart, C. J. S. "Race and Serial Killing in the Media: The Case of Wayne Williams." In *Speaking of Monsters*, edited by C. J. S. Picart and J. E. Browning (173–191). New York: Palgrave Macmillan, 2012. https://doi.org/10.1057/9781137101495_18.

"Police Shootings Database 2015–2021." *Washington Post*. Updated April 20, 2019. https://www.washingtonpost.com/graphics/investigations/police-shootings-database/.

Rosewood, Jack. *Jeffrey Dahmer: A Terrifying True Story of Rape, Murder & Cannibalism*. CreateSpace Publishing, 2017.

Serena, Katie. "The Gruesome Crimes of Albert Fish, the Brooklyn Vampire." All That's Interesting. October 30, 2020. https://allthatsinteresting.com/albert-fish.

Smith, Kevin D. "Civil Rights | Encyclopedia of Milwaukee." *Encyclopedia of Milwaukee*. 2016. https://emke.uwm.edu/entry/civil-rights/.

Swaine, Jon, Oliver Laughland, Jamiles Lartey, Kenan Davis, Rich Harris, Nadja Popovich, Kenton Powell, and the *Guardian* team. "The Counted: People Killed by Police in the United States – Interactive." *Guardian*. June 1, 2015. https://www.theguardian.com/us-news/ng-interactive/2015/jun/01/the-counted-police-killings-us-database.

"Violence Against the Transgender Community in 2020." Human Rights Campaign. 2020. https://www.hrc.org/resources/violence-against-the-trans-and-gender-non-conforming-community-in-2020.

Waldron, Lucas and Ken Schwencke. "Deadnamed." *ProPublica*. August 10, 2018. https://www.propublica.org/article/deadnamed-transgender-black-women-murders-jacksonville-police-investigation.

Walsh, Anthony. "African Americans and Serial Killing in the Media." *Homicide Studies* 9, no. 4 (2005): 271–291. https://doi.org/10.1177/1088767905280080.

Chapter 8: Sex

Baring, Jesse. *Perv: The Sexual Deviant in All of Us*. New York: Scientific American/Farrar, Strauss & Giroux, 2013.

Berg, Karl. *The Sadist*. Elektron, 2015. E-book.

Bovsun, M. "Mummified Head of Vampire of Düsseldorf — the Blood-Drinking Serial Killer — Displayed at Waterpark Haven Wisconsin Dells." *San Diego Union-Tribune*. July 6, 2018. https://www.sandiegouniontribune.com/business/tourism/ny-news-serial-killer-museum-wisconsin-20180706-story.html.

Brown, A. "On 22 August Sharon Lopatka Set Out to Look for Someone to Kill her." *Independent*. November 12, 1996. https://www.independent.co.uk/life-style/22-august-sharon-lopatka-set-out-look-someone-kill-her-so-she-posted-internet-message-discussion-group-alt-sex-necrophi-lia-want-talk-about-torturing-death-1351937.html.

Brown, George R. "Overview of Paraphilias and Paraphilic Disorders." *MSD Manual Consumer Version*. August 2019. https://www.msdmanuals.com/home/mental-health-disorders/sexuality-and-sexual-disorders/overview-of-paraphilias-and-paraphilic-disorders.

Dietz, P. E., R. R. Hazelwood, and J. Warren, "The Sexually Sadistic Criminal and His Offenses." *Bulletin of the American Academy of Psychiatry and the Law* 18, no. 2 (June 1990): 163–178. https://pubmed.ncbi.nlm.nih.gov/2372577/.

Dryden-Edwards, Roxanne. "Paraphilia (Sexual Disorders) Definition, Types, Treatment, Symptoms." MedicineNet. August 28, 2020. https://www.medicinenet.com/paraphilia/article.htm.

Gert H., J. R. Georgiadis, A. M. J. Paans, L. C. Meiners, F. H. C. E. van der Graaf, and A. A. T. Simone Reinders. "Brain Activation During Human Male Ejaculation." *Journal of Neuroscience* 23, no. 27 (2003): 9185-9193. https://doi.org/10.1523/JNEUROSCI.23-27-09185.2003.

Griffiths, Mark. "Stairing at the Rude Boys: A Brief Look at Climacophilia." Wordpress.com. December 16, 2016. https://drmarkgriffiths.wordpress.com/2016/12/16/stairing-at-the-rude-boys-a-brief-look-at-climacophilia/.

Harrison, M. A., E. A. Murphy, L. Y. Ho, T. G. Bowers, and C. V. Flaherty. "Female Serial Killers in the United States: Means, Motives, and Makings." *Journal of Forensic Psychiatry & Psychology* 26, no. 3 (2015): 383–406. https://doi.org/10.1080/14789949.2015.1007516.

"Impact of Child Abuse on Later Life: Crime Survey for England and Wales, Year Ending March 2016." Office for National Statistics. September 27, 2017. https://www.ons.gov.uk/peoplepopulationandcommunity/crimeandjustice/adhocs/007527impactofchildabuseonlaterlifecrimesurveyforenglandandwalesyearendingmarch2016.

Jackman, Tom and Troy Cole. *Rites of Burial*. Ward & Balkin Agency, 2012.

Kobayashi, J., B. D. Sales, and J. V. Becker, et al. "Perceived Parental Deviance, Parent-Child Bonding, Child Abuse, and Child Sexual Aggression." *Sex Abuse* 7 (1995): 25–44. https://doi.org/10.1007/BF02254872.

Krueger, R. B. "The DSM Diagnostic Criteria for Sexual Sadism." *Archives of Sexual Behavior*, 39, no. 2 (2010): 325–345. https://doi.org/10.1007/s10508-009-9586-3.

Levenson, J. and M. Grady. "The Influence of Childhood Trauma on Sexual Violence and Sexual Deviance in Adulthood." *Traumatology* 22, no. 2 (2016): 94–103. https://doi.org/10.1037/trm0000067.

Masters, Brian. *Killing for Company: The Case of Dennis Nilsen*. Arrow, 2020.

"Paraphilias Causes and Treatments." Mental Help. 2021. https://www.mentalhelp.net/sexual-disorders/paraphilias-causes-and-treatments/.

Slavin, M. N. et al. "Gender-Related Differences in Associations Between Sexual Abuse and Hypersexuality." *Journal of Sexual Medicine* 17, no. 10 (2020): 2029–2038. https://doi.org/10.1016/j.jsxm.2020.07.008.

Solakoglu O., N. Driver, and S. H. Belshaw. "The Effect of Sexual Abuse on Deviant Behaviors Among Turkish Adolescents: The Mediating Role of Emotions." *International Journal of Offender Therapy and Comparative Criminology* 62, no. 1 (2016). https://doi.org/10.1177/0306624X16642810.

Stuart, R. S. "Constructing Perversions: The DSM and the Classification of Sexual Paraphilias and Disorders." *Electronic Journal Human Sexuality* 15 (2012).

Swinney, C. L. *Monster: The True Story of Serial Killer Peter Kurten*. RJ Parker Publishing, 2016.

Weiner, Staci B. "Implications and Impact of Sexual Abuse on Children and Adolescents." Robson Forensic. May 11, 2020. https://www.robsonforensic.com/articles/child-sexual-abuse-psychology-expert/.

"What Causes Paraphilias?" International Society for Sexual Medicine. 2021. https://www.issm.info/sexual-health-qa/what-causes-paraphilias/?ref_condition=sexual-dysfunction.

Conclusion

Masters, Brian. *Killing for Company: The Story of a Man Addicted to Murder*. Arrow, 1995.

McCorristine, Shane. *William Corder and the Red Barn Murder.* Palgrave Macmillan UK, 2014.

Zuk, Marlene and Hamish G. Spencer. "Killing the Behavioral Zombie: Genes, Evolution, and Why Behavior Isn't Special." *BioScience*, vol. 70, no. 6 (2020), 515–520, https://doi.org/10.1093/biosci/biaa042.

About the Authors

HANNAH MAGUIRE and **SURUTHI BALA** are co-hosts of the smash hit true crime podcast *RedHanded*, which offers a weekly dose of murder, wit, and WTFs delivered with facts, anecdotal tangents, serious scrutiny, and real British flavor. *RedHanded* prides itself on looking past sensational headlines and getting to the truth of every murder, cult, and serial killer.